PRISON VIOLENCE

Getting "smart on crime" requires attention to prison violence. Levan makes an important contribution through her comprehensive review of the harm (to individuals, families and communities) and numerous research-based solutions.

Paul Leighton, Eastern Michigan University, USA

A compelling and comprehensive examination of a commonly overlooked subject. Particularly useful for newcomers to this area, the text is highly readable. While focusing on the United States, cross-national data is also presented, giving a comparative perspective. It also offers an astute discussion of ways to prevent and respond to prison violence.

Tiffany Bergin, Cambridge University, UK

In her compelling text, Dr Levan offers a comprehensive treatment of the age-old problem of prison violence, an issue that has remained in the shadows for far too long. Prison Violence: Causes, Consequences, and Solutions *provides a concise, yet detailed, analysis of the origins and implications of a prison culture that endorses violence as a means of currency and problem resolution. Levan brings a fresh and much-needed approach to the complex issue, incorporating cross-cultural comparisons and discussing the ways in which violence is dealt with inside the prison walls. A must read for students of penology and violence, as well as the public as a whole.*

Danielle Lavin-Loucks, Valparaiso University, USA

Solving Social Problems

Series Editor:
Bonnie Berry, Director of the Social Problems Research Group, USA

Solving Social Problems provides a forum for the description and measurement of social problems, with a keen focus on the concrete remedies proposed for their solution. The series takes an international perspective, exploring social problems in various parts of the world, with the central concern being always their possible remedy. As such, work is welcomed on subjects as diverse as environmental damage, terrorism, economic disparities and economic devastation, poverty, inequalities, domestic assaults and sexual abuse, health care, natural disasters, labour inequality, animal abuse, crime, and mental illness and its treatment. In addition to recommending solutions to social problems, the books in this series are theoretically sophisticated, exploring previous discussions of the issues in question, examining other attempts to resolve them, and adopting and discussing methodologies that are commonly used to measure social problems. Proposed solutions may be framed as changes in policy, practice, or more broadly, social change and social movement. Solutions may be reflective of ideology, but are always pragmatic and detailed, explaining the means by which the suggested solutions might be achieved.

Also in the Series

Prison Violence
Causes, Consequences and Solutions

KRISTINE LEVAN
Plymouth State University, USA

ASHGATE

04/16/14
LN
$59.95

© Kristine Levan 2012

Published by
Ashgate Publishing Limited
Wey Court East
Union Road
Farnham
Surrey, GU9 7PT
England

Ashgate Publishing Company
Suite 420
101 Cherry Street
Burlington
VT 05401-4405
USA

www.ashgate.com

British Library Cataloguing in Publication Data
Levan, Kristine.
   Prison violence : causes, consequences and solutions. – (Solving social problems)
   1. Prison violence–United States. 2. Prison violence–Canada. 3. Prison violence–Great Britain. 4. Prison violence–Prevention. 5. Prison violence–Psychological aspects. 6. Punishment in crime deterrence–Public opinion.
   I. Title II. Series
   365.6'41-dc23

Library of Congress Cataloging-in-Publication Data
Levan, Kristine.
   Prison violence : causes, consequences, and solutions / by Kristine Levan.
      p. cm. – (Solving social problems)
   Includes bibliographical references and index.
   ISBN 978-1-4094-3390-3 (hardback : alk. paper) – ISBN 978-1-4094-3391-0 (ebook)
   1. Prison violence. I. Title.
   HV9025.L48 2012
   365'.641--dc23

                                                                            2012020717

ISBN 978-1-4094-3390-3 (hbk)
ISBN 978-1-4094-3391-0 (ebk – PDF)
ISBN 978-1-4094-7177-6 (ebk – ePUB)

Printed and bound in Great Britain by the MPG Books Group, UK.

This book is dedicated to all of my mentors, in both my professional and personal life. It is also dedicated to the inmates and the families of inmates who have been affected by prison violence.

Contents

List of Figures and Tables

Figures

Tables

Chapter 1

An Introduction to Prisons, Punishment and Prison Violence

Introduction

The number of individuals residing behind bars has reached record numbers in many countries, including the United States. In 2009, there were more than 9.8 million individuals incarcerated worldwide (Walmsley 2009), more than 2 million of which were incarcerated in the United States (Glaze 2010). For myriad of reasons, prison and jail populations, as well as probation and parole populations, have increased in the last several decades.

It may seem relatively simple for communities to gloss over these facts. After all, as so many seem to believe, if someone has done the crime, they should do the time. Prisons are meant to be places for punishment, where people who have committed offenses against society are placed until they have served their prescribed amount of time. To add insult to injury, prisons are also often built in rural areas, far isolated from mainstream society, further removing them from the minds of the members of the free society, as well as from opportunities for their families and friends to visit with them while they are serving time.

Although the public seems to be willing to forget about these offenders once they are no longer members of the free community, at some point, they will likely need to contend with these individuals again. In fact, approximately 95 percent of those who are incarcerated will eventually return to free society (Hughes, Wilson and Beck 2001, as cited in Petersilia 2003). If facilities were indeed "correcting" people, the perfect transition would mean they are returning to these communities rehabilitated and ready to be reintegrated as law-abiding and contributing members of society.

However, the reality is far from this idea. Former prisoners are likely to carry their experiences from prison back to their respective communities. Not only are prisons ill-equipped and underfunded to provide programs and services to help these inmates become rehabilitated, they also expose inmates to a world of violence that has significantly negative effects on the individual. Even prisoners who were incarcerated for nonviolent offenses often acquire violent tendencies from exposure to a world where violence is the norm. This possibility becomes even more disheartening when factoring in the reality that most individuals admitted to prison are nonviolent offenders, including property and drug offenders, as well as those who have violated the terms of their parole for a technical violation (Austin and Irwin 2012). Victims who experience both physical and sexual violence while incarcerated report personal damages, such as physical injuries, suicidal tendencies, persistent nightmares, anger and contraction of sexually transmitted diseases.

The obvious victims of prison violence are the direct victims themselves. Victims suffer from physical and emotional damage done to them at the hands of their aggressors. Secondary victims, however, often include family members, such as spouses and children, who not only must cope with and survive a loved one or parent being incarcerated, but then must also confront the resulting individual who returns to them from this mysterious world of violence. Additionally, if the correctional system and its institutions are producing more damaged individuals than who were originally sent to serve their sentences, the community members become another secondary and indirect victim. Those who do not become rehabilitated as a result of serving time will almost certainly return to a life of crime, perhaps even crimes that are more violent or cause more financial damage than their original offenses. Members of society are the ones who potentially suffer from continued victimization at the hands of those who are released as more angry, more damaged, and more crime-prone than they were before.

The answer seems simple enough: reduce prison violence so that these individuals are not becoming more problematic to their families, communities and society at large. However, as researchers and practitioners alike will attest to, the solutions are infinitely more complicated. The world of incarceration is one that endorses various forms of violence, both from other prisoners and from correctional staff. Violence is seen as an acceptable and normal means of conflict resolution among inmates, causing what often begin as minor disagreements to erupt into major assaults, homicides or riots. Sexual violence and coercion are used as bargaining chips and currency. Membership to a gang is often seen as necessary for personal protection and survival. Correctional staff may resort to either actual violence or threats of violence in order to achieve the goal of control in a correctional facility. The "us versus them" mentality between correctional officers and inmates is a continuous and underlying theme in virtually all forms of communication. In short, violence is not only accepted, but has indeed become expected among both prisoners and correctional staff. Therefore, successfully reducing prison violence means disentangling the convict code and disrupting the prison culture at its very core.

In order to understand the contribution that prison culture has on the existence of violence, we must first understand what this culture entails. The National Institute of Corrections (2003) defines culture as "the values, assumptions and beliefs people hold that drive the way people think and behave" (Byrne, Hummer and Taxman 2008: 139). For prisons, this culture is defined not only by the prisoners themselves, but also by the correctional staff and administration, policy makers, and even the public.

The issue is further exacerbated by the fact that a great deal of violence goes undetected or unreported. Inmates are not likely to "snitch" on fellow inmates for fear of retaliation either by the perpetrator, or the perpetrator's associates, an issue that has been made more problematic with the rise of the prison gang culture. They are also not likely to report alleged infractions perpetrated by prison staff for fear of unofficial extra-legal punishment, or the belief that nothing will be done by prison administrators. For sexual victimization, these issues, as well as feelings of embarrassment or shame, often guide the decision to not report. In a subculture where masculinity is paramount, admitting to any victimization, and specifically sexual victimization, at the hands of another male, equates to a further loss of self-esteem in the eyes of an inmate. Ultimately, official accounts of violence are highly problematic indicators of the actual amount of violence that occurs inside the prison walls. Inmates are unlikely to report, prison officials may be unlikely to take action, and the official reports may be highly skewed toward those perpetrators who are viewed as most problematic by officials, such as those who are frequently punished in solitary confinement or who are known and active gang members.

Many years ago, Erving Goffman (1961) coined the term "total institution" to describe prisons. Every aspect of an inmate's life is controlled, including where they sleep, what time they eat their meals, and with whom they can interact while they are incarcerated. Because they are under control of the State, all their basic necessities, such as food, clothing and shelter, are provided for them. Because they live at least a portion of their lives out in these total institutions, is the government, then, not also responsible for their safety and health? How much responsibility does the state have in protecting them from harm, and when harm does come to them, what is the best manner in which to deal with the effects?

The Prison Experience

The first time someone visits a prison, they may be overwhelmed by feelings of fear for their personal safety. Often, this fear quickly subsides and gives way to a flood of other emotions. For me, the most striking emotion is that of despair.

My personal experiences in conducting research and performing other activities within prisons always end with me leaving the facility feeling a great sense of despair. This emotion is not unique to any one state or security level, nor is it exclusive to either male or female facilities. The feeling of despair cannot be adequately described with mere words. Numerous inmates have described to me their feelings of loss: loss of family relationships, loss of self-esteem, loss of feeling safe, and, perhaps the most essential, loss of freedom. I believe that my own personal feelings of despair result from the compassion that I feel for their sense of loss and, in some cases, their sense of hopelessness. Moreover, I am constantly reminded that before these individuals became inmates, before they became institutionalized, society considered them people.

The feeling of someone not being considered a person due to their actions, no matter how criminal those actions might be, seems inexcusable. Though I do believe in individuals being punished for their wrongdoing, I don't believe in them being over-punished for their wrongdoing. The system of punishment, as it currently exists, is one that not only condones prescribing (often overly extended) prison sentences, but also in subjecting inmates to extra legal punishment. Prison violence is nothing short of an extra legal punishment that serves to further dehumanize its victims.

Why Do We Punish?

This is the question at the root of any form of sanction, ranging from traffic citations to capital punishment. Each punishment carries with it an underlying purpose, but when examining corrections, there are five basic and generally accepted goals:

- Restitution – The focus of restitution is on the repayment to the victim or the community for financial losses incurred from a crime. This goal may be accomplished through payment of fines or fees, or returning monies directly to the victim, sometimes as reimbursement for counseling or medical treatment.
- Incapacitation – Incapacitation is the act of physically preventing offenders from committing additional crimes against the public. Although the immediate thought for incapacitation efforts are toward imprisonment, other sanctions, such as house arrest and electronic monitoring, may also achieve this purpose by removing offenders from the free society.
- Retribution – This is often used synonymously with just deserts. Retributive arguments center on serving sentences as a punishment for crime. These ideals are often found in punitive catchphrases, such as "you do the crime ... you do the time". The retributive philosophy dates back to the idea behind lex talionis, or "an eye for an eye" philosophy. Punishments that involve just deserts and retribution often walk a fine line between serving their purpose, and revenge.
- Deterrence – Deterrence is a goal that is often used without knowledge of its true meaning. Key to understanding the value of deterrence is in recognizing the difference between specific and general deterrence. Specific deterrence is the effects of punishment on the individual, and it states that punishing an offender will make them think twice before recidivating. General deterrence would argue that those in the community are deterred from crime when they observe offenders being punished for similar offenses. Deterrence will be discussed in more detail in Chapter 4, but the theoretical underpinnings demonstrate that for a punishment to deter, it must be 1) severe, 2) swift AND 3) certain. If all three tenets cannot be fulfilled, then deterrence cannot be achieved.
- Rehabilitation – A wide array of programming may be included in discussions of rehabilitation, including drug and alcohol treatment, mental health and behavioral treatment, education, vocational training, and any other activity that is meant to make the offender "whole". The ultimate goal

of most rehabilitation efforts is to allow the offender to return to society and reintegrate into their community without future crime commission.

Can a correctional system accomplish all five of these goals? Perhaps a carefully crafted system that individualizes punishment could, but many modern systems tend to rely on a "one size fits all" approach. Recent decades have shown a shift away from rehabilitation, and toward a system that emphasizes incapacitation and retribution. As prescribed sentences continue to increase, restitution has increased among low-level property offenders. Deterrence is the one goal that stands out as truly difficult to achieve, yet is the one that policy makers and correctional administrators often tout as being accomplished by the punitive stance on crime control. The basic tenets cannot be achieved under many modern correctional systems, including that of the United States. Although sanctions can accomplish the severity aspect, the other two aspects are more problematic. Swiftness is difficult due to overburdened court systems, creating a significant waiting period for trials. Certainty is difficult to achieve by the range of potential sentences for each offense, as well as the existence of plea bargains. The very fact that half of all crimes go unreported greatly reduces the certainty that an offender will be captured by law enforcement or prosecuted within the court system.

The History of Punishment

Early punishments relied almost exclusively on capital and corporal punishments and, in some instances, monetary fines. The Code of Hammurabi, for example, prescribed death as the default punishment for many offenses including adultery, breaking and entering, kidnapping, and making false accusations. The Covenant Code and the Massachusetts Body of Liberties followed suit. Part of this reliance on capital and corporal punishment was due to widespread beliefs in deterrence and retribution as primary goals. Although it was originally believed that public punishments, such as hanging and flogging, would help prevent the public from committing similar offenses, over time, some audience members began to feel sympathy toward the accused. Part of the issue also lies in the absence of a physical penitentiary system. Other than the occasional temporary holding cell, a formal correctional system was yet to be established.

In the United States, the creation of the Auburn and Pennsylvania prison systems signaled a significant shift in how punishment was perceived. Creators of these prison systems believed that inmates could be rehabilitated, though the implementation of these methods seems to have missed the mark. The result of these harsh systems was that the offenders' problems were actually often exacerbated, as is seen by inmates having psychological issues associated with solitary confinement and a lack of socialization and human interaction, as enforced by a mandated code of silence. Correctional systems have undergone a series of changes and transformations over time. Some eras tout increasing the work ethic of prisoners by increasing prison industry. The rehabilitation era heralded an increased emphasis on treatment and educational programming. A lack of quick results from rehabilitation efforts resulted in society becoming frustrated and disheartened. As the retributive era began in the 1980s, the focus began to shift toward becoming more punitive and retributive, and less on allowing the inmates to make reparations or become rehabilitative.

As of the publication of this book, the United States and other nations seem to remain focused on this retributive stance. Harsh, overcrowded conditions and a general lack of treatment and rehabilitation programs characterize the modern correctional landscape. Many seem to have given up hope on those who are sent to prison, assuming that a lifetime of recidivism awaits their release from prison. But, can any less truly be expected when inmates are confined in these conditions for extended periods of time?

Organization of this Book

The next chapter of this book will examine why the United States prison population has been increasing in the past few decades. Specifically, I will look at how American prisons and their populations have changed over time, as the government began to wage its War on Drugs and started to take a tougher approach toward all types of offenders. American prisons have become grossly overpopulated. This increase in the prison population is disproportionately comprised of substance abusers, females, minorities, gang members, sex offenders, the elderly and the mentally ill. This shift in the demographic makeup of the prison population has created challenges for which the nation has simply not been prepared. As a result, not only has the overall cost of corrections increased, so has the cost per inmate. In order to cope with an ever increasing and costly prison population, we have also seen an increasing reliance on privatized prisons. As the government-run facilities become grossly overcrowded, private companies have been more than eager to house inmates in order to turn a profit. I also discuss the unique issues surrounding confinement of illegal immigrants who are being detained, another population that has increased in recent years.

Chapter 3 looks at what we know about prison violence in comparison with other countries. Cross-national comparisons are difficult and problematic. They are ultimately important to understanding the larger picture with respect to prison populations and prison violence. A broad range of nations were selected for examination, including Canada, England and Wales, Scotland, Australia and New Zealand, Russia, South Africa, Germany, the Netherlands, Belgium, France, Italy, Sweden and Finland, Israel, China and Japan. Prison populations, rates, and, when available, conditions for prison violence are discussed for each country.

Chapter 4 will examine various explanations of prison violence. I discuss traditional correctional philosophies, such as the process of prisonization, the importation and deprivation theories, the idea of the prison hierarchy, and the convict code's place in understanding prison violence. I also contrast the theoretical explanations for violence among the female prison population with the male prison population. Then, general criminological theories of violence will be applied to understanding the nature of prison violence. Although prison populations often provide an ideal avenue to explain criminological theories, the existing literature on this topic is scarce. I explore how theories such as deterrence, routine activities, social bond, techniques of neutralization, anomie and strain, subculture, learning and labeling theory can be applied to help us understand prison violence more thoroughly. I also include a discussion of violence that occurs in extreme (and rare) circumstances, such as during riots and escapes, as well as among political prisoners, using the detainees in Guantanamo Bay and Palestinians held in Israeli prisons as examples.

The micro-level and macro-level effects of prison violence are discussed in detail in Chapter 5. Prisons and prisoners, though far removed from mainstream society, do not operate in a vacuum, and this chapter will examine the far-reaching effects of both incarceration and violence. Aside from the direct victim, I also explain the effects that incarceration and violence has on the victim's family, community and society as a whole. I also look specifically at how re-entry and reintegration can be interrupted or prevented by exposure to violence while incarcerated.

Chapter 6 explores why prison violence is such a complicated issue to understand. With inmates being hesitant or unlikely to report offenses committed against them, researchers and prison administrators have a difficult task to accomplish. Furthermore, correctional staff and institutions have historically taken a disinterest in providing solutions for violence among the incarcerated population. The public fuels this fire with a general lack of interest, or an even more problematic vengeful attitude towards prisoners. Ultimately, public opinion is crucial to resolution of this issue, as members of society are key in policymaking. Public response is often shaped by the media's distortion of events, and media representations of both prisoners and prison violence are often inaccurate.

In some ways, we are leaps and bounds ahead of what we knew about this issue just a few decades ago. Chapter 7 looks at what is being done to prevent and educate on this topic. For example, The Prison Rape Elimination Act, which has been in place for under a decade, has been key in focusing attention on this issue. Within institutions, efforts such as peer-led and professional education for inmates, closed circuit television surveillance, formation of gang-free facilities, and increased correctional officer training have been introduced in recent years. If an individual has been victimized, the facility can also offer psychological and medical treatment. New initiatives have been implemented to deal with the increasing population of AIDS- and HIV-infected inmates. These are just a few of the methods discussed in the chapter, and I will explore the effectiveness of these and other initiatives.

Finally, Chapter 8 examines the potential future of prison violence. Building on the information provided in Chapter 7, I look at what the best practices may be for prevention and treatment of violence among inmate populations. Within facilities, segregation policies, treatment options, gang diversion programs and other initiatives will be explored. I also consider alternative methods, such as softening what has become a very "get tough on crime" approach that is fueling the overcrowding, and subsequent increase in violent victimization, in prisons. The benefits of increasing community-based corrections are also discussed. Increasing public awareness of this issue and the potentially devastating consequences, as well as the benefits to alternatives to prison, is a key step forward for decreasing prison violence.

Purpose of this Book

The purpose of this book is to provide a comprehensive look at prison violence. One of the difficulties in discussing a topic such as prison violence is that violence can take many forms. The definition of violence that will be used throughout this book is one that Her Majesty's Prison Service (2006) has provided: "any incident in which a person is abused, threatened, or assaulted. This includes an explicit or implicit challenge to their safety, welfare, or health. The resulting harm may be physical, emotional or psychological" (Edgar 2008). The obvious and most egregious acts of violence, such as homicides, group assaults and sexual assaults, can have devastating effects on the victims, their families, and communities. Other acts of violence, such as simple assaults, fistfights, robbery, threats, and verbal abuse are far more common (Cooley 1993, O'Donnell and Edgar 1998, Ross and Richards 2003), and can also be very damaging to the victims.

It should be noted that this book primarily focuses on individual level violence, as well as collective forms of violence on the micro-level, as perpetrated by groups or gangs. It will not focus on the macro-level collective forms of violence, such as riots and facility-wide disturbances, although this issue will be discussed briefly in Chapter 4. Furthermore, it will not focus on violence perpetrated between correctional staff and inmates. The notable exception to this is the violence that female inmates experience at the hands of male correctional staff. These issues have causes, consequences and potential solutions that are, in themselves, complex and worthy of additional study, thereby placing them beyond the scope of this book.

It is my hope that this book will help to garner more interest in this issue, as it is one that is serious and more influential than it may seem at first blush. Until prison violence becomes a larger public concern, it will continue to be a silent plague that causes detriment to victims, families, communities and society in the years ahead.

Chapter 2
Prison, by the Numbers

Introduction

When comparing incarcerated populations across the world, the United States certainly dominates, with a rate of 756 individuals incarcerated per 100,000 members of the population (Walmsley 2009). As of 2010, the total population of the United States under some form of correctional supervision was more than 7 million people. Although more than 5 million individuals included in this figure are under community supervision (either probation or parole), there are still 1,605,127 individuals who are incarcerated in either prisons or jails nationwide (Guerino, Harrison and Sabol 2011).

Incarcerated populations of other countries will be described in more detail in Chapter 3.

Although the U.S. population comprises only about 5 percent of the world's population, they contribute 25 percent of the world's incarcerated population (Shelden 2010). The staggering difference between the United States and the nation with the second leading number of incarcerated individuals (Russia, with a rate of 629), leads many to wonder why America has so many individuals under correctional supervision. Does the United States have more crime than these other countries? Does the country define more offenses as criminal than other countries? Is the United States simply a more punitive nation?

The Conservative Approach and the Religious Right

Some of the punishment philosophies described in Chapter 1 are closely aligned with conservative approaches. Deterrence, incapacitation and retribution are associated with individuals being held responsible for their wrongdoing. The origins of criminal law are also closely tied with religiosity. Although lex talionis originates from the Code of Hammurabi, the Bible also states "an eye for an eye, a tooth for a tooth". The original justifications for incarceration were also partially religious. Penitentiaries were so named because those serving time were supposed to be seeking penance and asking for forgiveness (Shelden 2010).

As society has progressed, the United States has touted the separation of church and state. But, how separate are these institutions? An individual swearing their honesty to God by placing their hand on a Bible accompanies providing testimony in court. Every piece of currency in circulation has "In God We Trust" visible on the front. When politicians run for office, their religious affiliation undoubtedly becomes a primary issue of concern to voters. One must ultimately question whether a true separation between church and state really exists. Even more important, is the level of influence religion plays in all aspects of American government, including the crime control and punishment philosophies.

Increasing Correctional Populations

As many are aware, the United States has been experiencing an increase in jail and prison populations for the last several decades. The number of correctional institutions has more than tripled in the past 25 years (Lawrence and Travis 2004). The explanation for this lies not in an increase in crime rates, which have been steadily declining in recent decades, but in an increase in the nation's punitiveness. Zero tolerance policies and harsher sentences have led to drastic increases in the number of individuals under the supervision of the criminal justice system. Not only does America incarcerate more violent offenders than other countries, but also more nonviolent offenders. This punitive stance is illustrated by the fact that the United States is the only industrialized country to incarcerate individuals for writing a bad check (Shelden 2010).

This change is not something that has happened overnight. Rather, it is a shift that has been culminating since the 1960s, when President Lyndon B. Johnson declared a "War on Crime". Many believe this decade spawned the widespread fear of crime that continues to be present in modern American society (Austin and Irwin 2012).

The 1970s were filled with changes in crime control policies. In part due to a continued fear of crime from the public, more funds began to be allocated toward crime prevention and in investing in increasing policing efforts (Austin and Irwin 2012). Rehabilitation efforts, once heavily touted as revolutionary, were called into question when it was claimed, "the rehabilitative efforts that have been reported so far have had no appreciable effect on rehabilitation" (Martinson 1974: 25). Not surprisingly, sentencing models also began to shift toward an increased use of determinate sentences, allowing less judicial discretion in prescribing sentence length. The nexus of the public's attitude toward crime, when combined with increased sentencing and less emphasis on rehabilitation, meant Americans were beginning to incarcerate people for longer periods of time, offer them fewer services while incarcerated and be less concerned for their long-term welfare. This time period may signal the beginning of the true shift in correctional ideologies. Deterrence and retributive viewpoints began to dominate the correctional landscape, heralding treatment, rehabilitation and reintegration as less important correctional goals.

Crime was on the decline in the 1980s. However, media portrayals of crime lead many in the public to believe that there was a crime epidemic (Kappeler and Potter 2005, Austin and Irwin 2012). The Reagan administration's "War on Drugs", fueled harsher sentences and a catchy "Just Say No" campaign directed at the nation's youth, practically guaranteeing that Americans would be more than willing to lock away substance abusers for lengthy sentences. However, the increase in the prison population would have little effect on the aggregated crime rates. Only about one-quarter of the major crime reduction in recent decades can be attributed to an increase in the prison population. The remaining 75 percent is due to larger societal and economic changes (Spelman 2000).

The beginning of the dramatic increase of the incarcerated population began in the 1990s, when a fear of crime seemed to be at its greatest level. High profile cases, such as the kidnapping and murder of Polly Klaas, fueled the fire for the public, politicians and the media to embrace even tougher penalties for offenders. Cases like this allowed for states, such as California, to pass some of the harshest sentencing legislation ever created, such as three-strikes legislation. Although many states have some version of three-strikes laws, the policy that was passed in California in the 1990s allowed for three-time felons, including those committing nonviolent felonies, to be mandated to serve between 25 years and life behind bars. Truth in sentencing laws, which require inmates to serve a prescribed amount of their sentence, often 85 percent, before they are eligible for parole have been implemented in many states. Policies such as these represent a further shift toward longer sentences, and have greatly contributed to the recent growth of the prison population.

Overcrowding issues are often temporarily solved by either increasing the capacity of existing prisons, or building more correctional facilities (Schoenfeld 2010, Lynch 2011). In May 2011, the situation in the California prison system had become grim enough that the Supreme Court handed down a decision stating that the overcrowded prison conditions are a violation of the Eighth Amendment's guarantee against cruel and unusual punishment. Within two years from the ruling, the prison population must be reduced by 137.5 percent. Justice Kennedy's majority opinion stated that the prisons, as they currently exist, have "no place in civilized society" (*Brown v. Plata* 2011). This Supreme Court ruling is monumental, as courts are not generally quick to intervene on issues involving prisoners' rights. In accordance with prior Supreme Court decisions, in order to qualify as an Eighth Amendment violation of cruel and unusual punishment, conditions must:

- Demonstrate a deliberate apathy to basic human needs (such as safety or medical care);
- Wantonly inflict unnecessary pain to the inmate;
- "Shock the conscience" of the court or violate general standards of decency; or
- Include punishment that is grossly disproportionate to the crime

Prison overcrowding is often cited as being the primary contributor of prison violence (Gaes and McGuire 1985, Pratt 2009, Hassine 2010). As prisons house inmates beyond their designed capacity, typical solutions are to either place numerous inmates in individual cells that were originally designed for one or two inmates, or to create makeshift dormitory-style housing in areas originally designed to be gymnasiums, cafeterias or other large spaces. The more inmates housed in a particular area, the greater the likelihood of psychological, physical and sexual victimization (Hagemann 2008, Woolredge and Steiner 2009, Hassine 2010). Increasing the sheer number of inmates also reduces the opportunities available to participate in educational, vocational and rehabilitation programs, as there are limited numbers of inmates who can participate in these programs (Hassine 2010).

The Evolving (Increasing) Costs of Corrections

With the adult prison population representing less than one-fifth of the total correctional population, many are surprised to learn that the annual cost of confinement for the United States is more than $70 billion (Austin and Irwin 2012). The cost per inmate varies greatly, according to the level of security the inmate requires, as well as healthcare costs and rehabilitative efforts. Recent estimates from California indicate that the average cost per inmate is approximately $47,000 per year, which represents an increase since 2000–2001 of about $19,500 annually (How much does it cost? 2009).

Although many cite the cost of treatment, rehabilitation and educational programs as the primary contributor to the extraordinary cost, this is simply not the case. As seen in Table 2.1, rehabilitation programs only comprise about $1,600 annually per inmate (on average). The cost of security makes up a significant portion of the total annual expenditures ($19,663), followed by health care ($12,442) (How much does it cost? 2009). Because of the recent increase in health-care costs, due in part to increases in the number of elderly inmates, as well as the cost of treated terminally ill offenders and pregnant female inmates, it is likely a safe assumption that medical expenses will continue to increase.

In contrast, financial losses from crime victimization are considerably lower than the cost to incarcerate those who have committed these offenses. For instance, in 2006, the total annual financial losses for the United States were about $18.4 billion. Victim expenses, including loss of time from work, medical expenses and loss of property are represented in this figure (Austin and Irwin 2012). Therefore, the United States spends more to punish those who have committed a crime than the actual act itself costs the victim and society.

The cost of incarceration becomes even more shocking when comparing it with other services. In both California and New York, more money is currently spent on incarcerating inmates than on education (Austin and Irwin 2012). It seems paradoxical that the public is more accepting of spending resources on punishment than they are on prevention through investment in services, such as education, which have been clearly correlated with a lower propensity to commit crime. Facts such as this are illustrative of the type of "knee jerk" reactions society often has to crime and criminals.

Table 2.1   Annual cost per inmate in California (2008–2009)

Expenditure Item	Cost per inmate
Security	**$19,663**
Medical Care	$8,768
Psychiatric Services	$1,928
Pharmaceuticals	$998
Dental Care	$748
Total Inmate Health Care	**$12,442**
Facility operations	$4,503
Classification services	$1,773
Maintenance of inmate records	$660
Reception, testing, assignment	$261
Transportation	$18
Total Operations	**$7,214**
Administration	**$3,493**
Food	$1,475
Inmate activities	$439
Inmate employment and canteen	$407
Clothing	$171
Religious activities	$70
Total Inmate Support	**$2,562**
Academic education	$944
Vocational training	$354
Substance abuse programs	$313
Total Rehabilitation Programs	**$1,612**
Miscellaneous	**$116**
Total	**$47,102**

Source: How much does it cost? 2009

http://www.lao.ca.gov/laoapp/laomenus/sections/crim_justice/6_cj_inmatecost.aspx

The Evolving Nature of the Prison Population

Substance Abusers

There is no question that the War on Drugs has resulted in an increase in the number of inmates who have an issue with substance abuse. Because drug crimes have been federalized, this increase has disproportionately affected federal prisons. Whereas only 18 percent of state inmates are serving a prison sentence for a drug related offense, over half of all federal inmates are serving time for a drug related offense (Guerino et al. 2011). These statistics only illustrate part of the issue, as many inmates serving sentences for violent or property crimes also have issues with substance abuse. As much as one-third of property offenders admit that their offense was committed in order to obtain money to purchase drugs (Mumola and Karberg 2006).

This dramatic increase in the substance abuse population is something that the American correctional system was unprepared for. Although 74 percent of prisons offer substance abuse treatment (Taxman Perdoni and Harrison 2007), "treatment" may encompass a wide range of services, with varying levels of participation and effectiveness (MacKenzie 2006). Because of the large number of inmates that need treatment, waiting lists are often extensive, meaning many who need drug treatment will not be able to participate (Harrison 2001, Petersilia 2003). Even those who are able to participate are often not exposed to treatment that has the frequency, intensity or duration needed to be effective (Harrison 2001).

Substance abusers who are not engaged in treatment programs that lead to successful rehabilitation pose particular problems to the safety and security of the institution. Inmates who are under the influence of drugs may suffer from severe pharmacological effects, which may include hallucinations and delusions. Additionally, many drug abusers continue to use substances behind bars, a practice that obviously violates official prison rules. Thus, these inmates often engage in buying substances from the prison black market, an environment that has become synonymous with prison violence.

Minority Populations

Recent decades have experienced a dramatic shift in the racial and ethnic backgrounds of the inmate population. In 1954, when the *Brown v. Board of Education* decision was handed down, African-Americans comprised 30 percent of the total prison population (Mauer 2006b). As the civil rights movement gained momentum throughout the 1960s and 1970s, the African-American prison population began to increase (Johnson 2006). By 2010, the rate of white male inmates was 456 per 100,000, while the rates for Hispanic and African-American inmates were 1,252 and 3,059, respectively (Guerino et al. 2011). Nationwide, it is estimated that an African-American male has a 29 percent chance of being imprisoned throughout his lifetime, but in Washington, D.C., 75 percent of

African-American males will be sentenced to either jail or prison throughout their lifetime (Mauer 2006b).

Major discrepancies in the rates of incarceration have been attributed to a multitude of factors. Criminal involvement is closely linked with factors such as unemployment, poverty and barriers to legitimate economic success. From a socioeconomic perspective, crime is most likely to occur in inner-city neighborhoods, which, due to a wide variety of factors, are more likely to have minorities as the primary residents. Because these neighborhoods have been identified as high crime areas, they are more likely to be actively patrolled by law enforcement. This differential policing means that those residing in these communities are more likely to be caught for their involvement in crime than those residing in more affluent neighborhoods.

There is no question that policies such as the War on Drugs and mandatory minimum sentences have disproportionately affected minorities (Mauer 2006b). One example of sentencing disparity can be seen in the differences in sentence severity between cocaine and crack cocaine. In the 1980s, Federal Sentencing Guidelines provided that the penalty for possessing a small amount of usable crack (5 grams) was equivalent to trafficking cocaine. Although the Fair Sentencing Act of 2010 alleviated some of the disparity associated with a crack possession charge, there is still a harsher penalty associated with crack, which is predominantly found in less affluent neighborhoods.

Although minority populations behind bars have increased, there has not been a proportionate increase in the number of minority correctional officers. Because prisons are often located in rural areas, potential officers may be reluctant to move to these areas, as it may mean isolating themselves from members of the same racial or ethnic backgrounds. Minorities may also be hesitant to become employed in a field that has historically had significant issues with discrimination (Camp, Saylor and Wright 2000). The disadvantage to being unable to hire a reasonable number of minority correctional officers is that there may be an even wider gap between the keeper and the kept. Inmates may have difficulty relating to officers who are from backgrounds different from their own. The end result is a more divisive culture between officers and prisoners, further hindering rehabilitation efforts, and perhaps even encouraging violence among the inmate population, as well as between the inmate and officer populations.

The increase in minority populations in the prison system has resulted in a community to prison pipeline for some neighborhoods. This issue will be discussed in more detail in Chapter 5. But, it should be understood that as minorities exit their communities en masse and enter prison, most eventually return to these communities. Those not involved in violent crime while in the community are likely to return more violent and criminogenic. Entering prison often means becoming immersed in a culture where race is the primary identifier, and in order to bond with others, inmates often join gangs that are formed along racial and ethnic lines.

Gangs

It is difficult to know exactly how many inmates are affiliated with gangs. One reason is because of the range of gang involvement across individual inmates. Some may be characterized as hard-core gang leaders, while others are either fringe members, or simply gang sympathizers, making true estimates of the number of gang members and the amount of violent activity attributed to these members problematic (Ruddell, Decker and Egley 2006). Additionally, there is a great deal of secrecy involved in gang membership, as simply being a member of a gang often entails sanctioning, such as being placed in administrative segregation. Gang membership varies by state, with Illinois estimating that approximately 90 percent of its correctional population is affiliated with a gang (Fleisher and Decker 2007). Other states indicate that less than 5 percent of their inmate population belongs to a gang (Trulson, Marquart and Kawucha 2006). Nationwide estimates indicate that about one-quarter of all inmates are members of a prison gang (Knox 2005).

From 1985 to 1992, known gang membership behind bars increased dramatically. In 1985, 12,624 inmates were affiliated with a gang, but by 1992, this number had risen to 46,190 (Fleisher and Decker 2007). These changes are, in part, due to changes in the sentencing of crimes that are typically closely associated with gang membership in the community. Most notably, the War on Drugs that has disproportionately affected minorities has also naturally disproportionately affected minority gang members. These increases are also due to high numbers of gang members in the community who commit violence and other crimes that ultimately result in a prison sentence. As of 2011, there were an estimated 1.4 million active gang members, including those in the community and in prison (Continuing Gang Threat 2011).

Inmates who are affiliated with gang pose particular problems for correctional staff and administration. More centralized and higher ranking gang members are more likely to be violent than fringe members of gangs (Gaes, Wallace, Gilman, Klein-Saffran and Suppa 2002). Members are more likely to directly commit violence while incarcerated (Scott 2001, Gaes et al. 2002, Drury and DeLisi 2011). In addition to engaging in violence, gangs and gang members are also likely to actively engage in the black market. The black market in prison controls all of the contraband, which may include weapons, drugs, cigarettes and alcohol. Because of the low supply of contraband, gang members often fill a need by providing these goods to fellow inmates, usually at inflated prices.

Muslims

While many inmates turn to gangs formed along racial or ethnic lines for protection from violence, others become more entrenched in religion as a coping mechanism. Although some do convert to non Judeo-Christian religions as a form of protection from other inmates, most do so in an effort to find meaning or identity in their lives (Hamm 2008). Conversion to the Muslim religion while incarcerated combined with an increased likelihood for Muslims to become incarcerated due to the increased punitiveness against Muslims as a result of the War on Terror, has led to an increase in the number of Muslims who are currently serving time behind bars. Islam has become the religion that is the fastest growing of all religions among prisoners (Hamm 2008). In 2003 Muslims comprised as much as 20 percent of the prison population (Waller 2003).

In extreme and rare examples, terrorists have been able to recruit prisoners as pawns in their quest to overthrow the United States government. This is certainly the exception and not the rule, as most convert and then use their religion as a primary motivator for rehabilitation (Hamm 2008).

The increasing number of Muslim prisoners is certainly not unique to the United States. In England and France, for instance, Muslims represent an increasing sector of the prison population. English prisons are experiencing an increase in the formation of gangs that are religiously affiliated, especially among Muslims (Phillips 2012). Among French prisoners, Muslims comprise the greatest number of inmates, even though they only represent 10 percent of the population in the general community (Simon and De Waal 2009). Due to fear of Islamic extremism, prison guards in France are now trained in detecting warning signs associated with extremism (Simon and De Waal 2009).

Sex Offenders

In 1980, there were approximately 20,500 sex offenders serving time in state prisons. By 2009, this number had increased dramatically to approximately 167,000 sex offenders. Approximately 67,600 were serving time for rape, and about 99,400 for other forms of sexual assault (Guerino et al. 2011). These numbers indicate that the number of inmates serving time in a state correctional facility has increased by more than eightfold, and they now comprise more than 12 percent of the total state prison population.

A complex set of circumstances has led to this increase. The first is the evolution in legal definitions of sexual offenses. Until the 1960s, the only sexual offenses acknowledged by the law were rape (forced heterosexual penetration) and sodomy (consensual homosexual penetration). Sexual offenses have been further expanded and make additional discrepancies to include acts such as public indecency, statutory rape and the broader category of sexual assault. Although the prevalence of sexual offending may not have increased per se, the inclusion of these additional classifications of sexual acts has resulted in many more inmates being classified as sex offenders.

Furthermore, victims of sexual offenses have historically been reluctant to report the crime to law enforcement for a variety of reasons. Victims, who often know their assailant, indicate a fear of retaliation, embarrassment, a belief that the assailant may not be caught, of a fear of the criminal justice processes as potential reasons to not report. Although only about half of sexual offenses are reported to the police (Truman 2011), this represents an increase over the past few decades.

This may be due to advances in DNA technology, passage of rape shield laws and less stigmatization toward the victims than in years past.

Prescribed sentences for sex offenders have remained relatively stable over time. The maximum sentence for rape is 154 months, and for sexual assault 90 months. Murder is the only offense for which longer sentences are given (Sourcebook of Criminal Justice Statistics 2004). Although the sentence given has essentially remained unchanged, the actual time served has increased. The "get tough" approach that has resulted in three strikes and truth in sentencing legislation has affected sex offender population. Other legislation specifically targets sex offenders. One example is the Jessica Lunsford Act, which requires a mandatory minimum sentence for anyone who commits a sexual offense against a child under the age of 12.

The increase in the sex offender population in prisons creates unique issues. Those who are identified as sex offenders are more likely to be violently victimized by other inmates, as will be discussed in more detail in Chapter 4. Predatory inmates label them as targets for physical and sexual violence. Because sexual offenses comprise a wide range of actions, they are also a difficult group to provide treatment to in an effective manner. Limitations and recommendations for treatment options are also explored in later chapters. There is no question that the increase in this subgroup creates additional dissention among the inmate population, as well as rehabilitation challenges.

Female Inmates

Women make up a relatively small proportion of the total inmates in the United States, comprising approximately 15 percent of the total institutional population, or 198,600 inmates (Glaze 2010). Although only a fraction of the total population, the number of women who are under correctional supervision, either in the community or in an institution, has been increasing rapidly in the past few decades. This trend has been experienced in North America, Western Europe and Latin America (Reynolds 2008). The Netherlands, a country that historical enjoyed low levels of incarceration (see Chapter 3), has also seen a dramatic increase in their female prison population. Between 1995 and 2005, their rate of incarceration nearly doubled, from 420 to 816 (Van Gemmert 2002, Slotbloom, Bijleveld, Day and Van Giezen 2008, as cited in Slotbloom, Kruttschnitt, Bijleveld and Menting 2011).

The War on Drugs in America has disproportionately affected females, especially minority females. One of the differences noted between male and female drug arrestees is that females are more likely to commit drug sales for economic survival, in part as a result of their exclusion or denial of equal pay in the legitimate job market (Richie 2002). Females are less likely to engage in violence than males, and their involvement in violence is often in connection with a male counterpart. For instance, females often join gangs because of their significant others' involvement in gangs (Trammell 2012).

This trend affects populations of other nations as well as the United States. As a result of the punitive efforts directed at illegal substances, the borders of the country are more closely watched than ever before, increasing the possibility of arrest (Reynolds 2008). Those attempting to cross a nation's border with an illegal substance are therefore more likely to be caught, arrested and sanctioned.

Changes in the sentencing guidelines have also disproportionately affected females. For instance, the indeterminate sentencing structure that once guided judicial discretion allowed for factors such as abuse or custodial parenthood to allow for more lenient sentences for some offenders. This structure has been all but abandoned in an attempt to reduce sentencing disparity. However, because females are more likely than their male counterparts to have suffered from abuse, and are more likely to be the primary custodial parents, the move toward determinate sentences and mandatory minimums places female offenders and their dependent children at a disadvantage (Chesney-Lind 2002).

Women have been called "forgotten offenders" for many reasons (Chesney-Lind 2002). In addition to their small numbers within the correctional population, they also tend to not cause trouble while incarcerated, making it easier for correctional staff and policy makers to overlook their unique needs (Chesney-Lind 2002). As a result, female inmates are often given less access to correctional programming, such as education, vocational opportunities and therapeutic interventions.

An example of these disparities can be seen in the state of New Hampshire, by comparing the opportunities afforded to male inmates in the Concord prison, versus those provided to female inmates in Goffstown, the only female facility in the state. In Concord, male inmates can choose from vocational programs, including upholstering, woodworking, culinary arts and auto mechanics. In contrast, women are given basic word processing training and provided with three sewing machines in a small room. According to a report by the New Hampshire Advisory Committee to the U.S. Commission on Civil Rights, in the past 20 years, only two female inmates have obtained a high school diploma while incarcerated (Love 2011).

Discrepancies in opportunities are certainly not unique to New Hampshire. The rapid growth of the female inmate population is an unintended consequence of harsh policies set forth in the United States, as well as other nations. As a result, many facilities have few options on the best way to manage these populations. The compounding effects of "get tough" sentencing policies means that we are imprisoning women, many of whom have psychological and substance abuse issues, without providing them with adequate treatment and rehabilitation options. The lack of programming can have devastating effects on the female prison population. As will be discussed in more detail in Chapter 4, lack of access to programs, services and treatment can result in increases in violence among the inmate population.

Elderly Inmates

In the United States, the population of older inmates has increased by approximately 10,000 per year since 1995 (Aday 2003). Mandatory minimum sentences and truth-in-sentencing laws have greatly contributed to this increase, as more individuals are serving lengthier prison sentences and are aging behind bars. Others are arrested, primarily for nonviolent sex offenses, later in their lives. Approximately a third of older inmates have been convicted of a sexual offense (Flynn 2000).

This phenomenon is also not unique to the U.S. For instance, in the U.K., the older prison population has also grown substantially. Those age 60 and over are the fastest growing age demographic (H.M. Inspectorate of Prisons 2005, as cited in Crawley and Sparks 2006). This increase in the U.K. is primarily due to an increase in the number of sex offender convictions (Crawly and Sparks 2006), which is likely a result of harsher penalties enacted against sex offenders.

Older inmates suffer the same maladies as older individuals living in the free community, such as deteriorated vision and hearing, mobility difficulties and a decline in their general health conditions. Encountering these difficulties while incarcerated can be especially problematic and some older inmates describe their period of incarceration as a "disaster" (Crawley and Sparks 2006: 69).

Inmates over the age of 60 are often either sex offenders or nonviolent offenders serving lengthy sentences, both of which have an increased likelihood to be violently victimized while incarcerated (Adams 1992, Dumond, 1992, Turner, Sundt, Applegate and Cullen 1995, Mariner 2001, Hensley, Tewksbury and Castle 2003). This, combined with the unique health obstacles of elderly inmates, has made them prime targets for violent victimization (Bowker 1980a, Vito and Wilson 1985, Chaneles 1987). Some states segregate older inmate populations into separate units or blocks, in part for their protection from being victimized by younger inmates (Aday 1994, 2003). This also makes it easier and more cost effective to deliver medical care to a multitude of individuals in a singular location.

Mentally Ill Inmates

In the 1970s, the movement toward deinstitutionalization of the mentally ill began. Many mental hospitals began closing, in part as a result of a Supreme Court ruling that stated that anyone who is determined to have a mental illness has the right to treatment (*Wyatt v. Stickney* 1972). This, coupled with more stringent policies standards for individuals to be committed (posing harm to themselves or others), means that many individuals who might formerly have been committed to a mental institution were now left unsupervised in the community (Sigurdson 2000, Toch and Kupers 2007). When comparing those housed in mental institutions with those in correctional facilities, three times as many inmates have been diagnosed with a serious mental illness as those housed in mental institutions (Lurigio and Snowden 2008). It has been estimated that between 10 and 20 percent of inmates have been diagnosed with a mental illness (Jemelka, Rahman and Trupin 1993, Lovell and Jemelka 1998, James and Glaze 2006, Lurigio and Snowden 2008).

Those who suffer from mental illness in the community may be more likely to engage in criminogenic behavior. This behavior need not be violent to capture the attention of law enforcement, ultimately resulting in a potential jail or prison sentence. The result of the deinstitutionalization, combined with changes in sentencing policies, has resulted in an increase in the number of inmates who have some form of mental disorder (Toch and Adams 1987, Kupers 1999, Toch and Kupers 2007). It has been estimated that as many as 15 percent of inmates suffer from at least one major mental illness, such as schizophrenia or major depression (Sigurdson 2000).

Despite this, very few inmates receive any form of mental health care while incarcerated and correctional officers have little to no training in dealing with the mentally ill (Lurigio and Snowden 2008). The reaction of a mentally ill inmate to the strain of being incarcerated ranges from isolating oneself in his or her own cell, to committing acts of violence against other inmates and/or correctional staff (Toch and Adams 1987). Recent research also links having a low IQ with involvement in prison violence (Diamond, Morris and Barnes 2012). Due to their poor communication skills or issues with paranoia, inmates with lower mental functioning often avoid joining a gang for protection (Rotter and Steinbacher 2001, Lurigio and Snowden 2008). Mentally ill inmates are at an increased risk of victimization when compared to more mentally stable inmates (Rotter and Steinbacher 2001, Lurigio and Snowden 2008).

Individuals committing violent infractions are often subjected to segregation units or solitary confinement, regardless of the condition of their mental health (Haney 2003, Lurigio and Snowden 2008). Moreover, punishments, including solitary confinement, are unlikely to serve as a deterrent to the inmates if they are unable to rationally comprehend consequences of their actions (Diamond et al. 2012). Meant as punishment, this type of housing may indeed perpetuate further acts of violence, as "the environment in this kind of unit often exacerbates psychiatric symptoms" (Toch and Kupers 2007: 15).

Private Prisons

Private prisons are those that the government contracts to be maintained and controlled by a third party. As prison overcrowding and increasing costs became more problematic in the 1980s, the nation began to more heavily rely on private prisons. More than 25,000 federal and more than 94,000 state inmates were housed in private facilities in 2010 (Glaze 2011), and nearly half of all immigrants detained by the federal government are held in private institutions (Banking on bondage 2011). These numbers represent an increase of approximately 1,600 percent since 1990 (Banking on bondage 2011). Thirty states currently maintain some portion of their inmate population at a private institution (Mason 2012).

The private prison industry is dominated by a few companies, with the two largest companies earning over $3 billion in revenue in 2010 (Banking on bondage 2011). For-profit prisons have a vested interest in keeping prison populations inflated. Corrections Corporation of America (CCA), the largest of these companies, is quoted in a report to the Securities and Exchange Commission as saying "The demand for facilities and services could be adversely affected by ... leniency in conviction or parole standards and sentencing practices" (Banking on bondage 2011).

Aside from the ethical dilemmas associated with profiting from another individual's misery, private prisons have recently been criticized for being costly and ineffective. Each inmate housed in private facilities costs as much as $1,600 more per year than those housed in public facilities. This figure is even more astounding given the trend in private institutions to select inmate who are less costly to house, such as those who have medical conditions (Oppel 2011). The result is that the inmates who are the most expensive are kept in public facilities, placing a greater financial burden on the government and, ultimately, the taxpayers.

If an inmate's success is measured by lower rates of recidivism, private prisons seem to fail in this aspect as well. Recently released inmates from private facilities are not less likely to recidivate than those released from public ones (Spivak and Sharp 2008). Therefore, inmates from private prisons will have at least as much difficulty as others in reintegrating back into their communities.

When compared with those of public prisons, employees of private prisons have lower salaries, fewer benefits and less training, leading to more staff turnover (Banking on bondage 2011, Mason 2012). The result of high levels of employee turnover is that there are fewer seasoned officers on duty and higher levels of stress among officers. This environment lends itself to increases in violence, as evidenced by private prisons having as many as double the number of assaults as public institutions (Mason 2012). Sexual assaults are also prevalent among private prisons. In 2007, the private prison in Torrance, New Mexico had one of the highest rates of sexual assault in the United States. In 2009, after numerous allegations of sexual abuse against female inmates perpetrated by correctional officers, both Hawaii and Kentucky removed their inmates from the privately run Otter Creek Correctional Center (Walshe 2012).

Illegal Immigrants

Illegal immigrant populations represent another growing population of inmates. The Immigration and Customs Enforcement (ICE), a division of the Department of Homeland Security, is responsible for housing illegal immigrants who are detained. The number of beds used exclusively for immigrant detention has grown from about 6,300 in 1996 to over 33,000; there are about 250 facilities in the United States, holding approximately 363,000 immigrants (Immigrant Detention). It costs as much as $60,590 per year to house a detainee, and the estimated costs for immigration detention for 2012 are approximately $2 billion (Immigrant Detention, U.S. Immigration).

The primary reason for the increase is due to an increase in border patrol enforcement. Illegal immigrant may be caught by authorities while committing a crime, or when attempting to enter the country illegally. It should be noted that of those who are in detention, many have never committed a criminal offense, and most of those are nonviolent offenses (Immigration Detention). Although much of the public maintains a fear of illegal immigrants and equates them with being violent criminals, these fears seem to be unfounded.

Poor prison conditions and inadequate medical care has been linked to the deaths of some detainees (Immigration Detention). According to statistics found on the ICE website, between October 2003 and December 2011, 127 deaths occurred while in custody. Some recorded causes of death among detainees include asphyxia, cancer, Hepatitis C, AIDS, brain injuries, cardiac arrest and natural causes, among many other reasons.

In a recent report, it was noted that ICE detention facilities have relatively low levels of sexual assault, with the exception of the El Paso Processing Center in Texas. This facility showed an inmate-on-inmate sexual assault rate of 2.1 percent, a rate that is approximate to the average rate among prisoners nationwide (Beck, Harrison, Berzofsky, Caspar and Krebs 2010). It should be noted that this survey was conducted in only five ICE facilities and included only 957 inmates. Considering the large number of illegal immigrants who are housed in detention facilities, these surveys should be given to a larger number of respondents.

The question remains how many assaults, injuries and deaths are occurring among detainees that are not included in official or unofficial numbers. In 2010, it was reported that ICE also maintain 186 unmarked and unlisted facilities for detainees, many of which are located in commercial building spaces. Of particular interest is the allegation that these facilities and their employees are not subject to the standards of official ICE detention facilities (Stevens 2010). Illegal immigrants who are detained and housed continue to be a population that is difficult to collect adequate information on, in part due to the shroud of secrecy that seems to surround their detention.

Conclusion

As the information from this chapter illustrates, the prison population is increasing, and the types of inmates being incarcerated has been changing over the past several decades. As will be discussed in Chapter 4, the characteristics and demographics of inmates are often predictive of their involvement in prison violence. For instance, older inmates, those with mental illnesses, and those convicted of sex offenses are commonly victims of violence, especially at the hands of younger inmates who may have more violent tendencies. Gang members, on the other hand, may be more likely to be violent than those not involved in a gang. The increase in the female prison population also poses issues, as few female facilities exist, and many of those that exist do not have the adequate space or funding to provide the necessary treatment or programming. Prison administrators are therefore faced with not only with overcrowded facilities, but also with housing special populations at levels that they have not had to contend with in the past. These populations bring their own unique issues, and levels of violence may increase as a result unless these circumstances are considered carefully.

When comparing the United States with many other nations, prison victimization rates generally fall in the average range. In the community, American citizens tend to be less likely to be victimized when it comes to property crimes. Examinations of violent crime paint a very different picture. For instance, when comparing homicide rates, the United States has a rate that is four times that of most nations in Western Europe (Mauer 2006a).

The increase in crime rates that occurred prior to the 1990s account for a very small portion of the increase in the prison population. According to Blumstein and Beck (1999), revisions in the nation's sentencing policies are responsible for 88 percent of the increase in the prison population (Mauer 2006a). The bulk of the prison population in the United States is comprised not of violent offenders, but of those who have committed a drug related offense. Since 1980, the numbers of individuals incarcerated for drug offenses has increased tenfold (Mauer 2006a). Drug sentences in the United States are more severe than those in other countries, but this is a trend that is true for sentencing for most types of offenses.

Chapter 3
Prisons and Prison Violence
in Other Countries

Introduction

Attempting to measure imprisonment rates cross-nationally is inherently flawed. Not only are different actions defined as criminal offenses in various countries, but also the specified sanctions for these crimes vary from monetary fines to capital punishment (Pease 1991, 1992, 1994, as cited in Cavadino and Dignan 2006). Other issues, such as whether pre-trial detainees, general jail populations and juveniles are included in the official numbers, also make comparisons problematic (Walmsley 2009).

Despite these difficulties, it is of utmost importance to attempt to make these cross-country comparisons. Conditions that exist in one country that promote violence among inmates are likely to exist in other countries with similarly situated inmate populations. Understanding the number of individuals who are incarcerated in each country is also important. When examining predictors of violence among the incarcerated population, the singular characteristic that may be the most predictive of violence is institutional overcrowding (Gaes and McGuire 1985). It has been noted that the rates of imprisonment are the highest in countries with the most extreme levels of income inequality, such as the United States. Even when making within country comparisons, individual states with more income inequality also have higher rates of imprisonment. Within the United States, for example, states with the highest rates of incarceration are Texas, Louisiana, Mississippi, Alabama and California (Wilkinson and Pickett 2009, as cited in Austin and Irwin 2012).

When comparing the United States to other countries (see Table 3.1), the differences are obvious. The rate of incarceration in the United States is much greater, leading to overcrowding in correctional facilities, and ultimately contributing to a prevalence of prison violence. Many of the conditions of punishment that exist in the United States, such as capital punishment, solitary confinement, overcrowding and strip searches, have been condemned by the European Court of Human Rights (Snacken 2010, as cited in Ross 2011). Because Article 3 of the European Convention on Human Rights states that "no one shall be subjected to torture or inhuman or degrading treatment or punishment", Ross (2011) argues that the deplorable conditions of the prisons may prevent some countries from being willing to extradite American citizens back to the United States (158).

Table 3.1   Comparative incarceration rates by country

Country	Number of inmates	Rate of incarceration (per 100,000)
United States	2,293,157	756
Russia	891,738	629
South Africa	164,297	335
Israel	22,788	326
New Zealand	7,887	185
England/Wales	83,392	153
Scotland	7,893	152
Australia	27,615	129
China	1,565,771	119
Canada	38,348	116
The Netherlands	16,416	100
France	59,665	96
Belgium	10,002	93
Italy	55,057	92
Germany	73,203	89
Sweden	6,770	74
Finland	3,370	64
Japan	81,255	63

Source: Based on data drawn from Walmsley 2009

Canada

Although Canada shares a border, as well as several common characteristics with the United States, the prison population demonstrates some major differences. The most recent population counts show that Canada has 38,348 incarcerated offenders, a number that is strikingly different from that of the United States. This discrepancy is even more pronounced when considering that youthful offenders are included in Canada's prison statistics (Walmsley 2009). Unlike the United States, which is divided into state and federal institutions, all Canadian prisons are considered federal institutions and exclusively house offenders who are serving sentences of more than two years. The average sentence served is approximately 46 months, and the most frequently cited offenses among Canadian prisoners include robbery, drug related offenses, assault and rape or sexual assault (Simon and De Waal 2009).

Between 1990 and 1999, Ontario prisons experienced a total of 13 homicides (Wobeser, Datema, Bechard and Ford 2002, as cited in Sattar 2004). However, when comparing across provinces, and across time, a very different picture emerges. In 1967, homicide rates for Canadian prisoners were 14 per 100,000. By 1979, this number had risen to 118 per 100,000 prisoners (Porporino, Doherty and Sawatsky 1987, as cited in Sattar 2004).

When compared to the United States, Canadian prisons do not experience high levels of sexual assault. The Correctional Services of Canada do not currently keep statistical records of incidents of sexual assault among prisoners, so it is difficult to estimate how many instances occur (Ellenbogen 2009). The differences in the culture between the two nations may explain some of the discrepancies. America is a very individualistic country, where one's status is of utmost importance. Individual status becomes even more important once incarcerated, and some engage in sexual violence to assert their dominance and achieve a higher status than their fellow prisoners. Canadian citizens simply do not exhibit this competitive attitude, so it is therefore not likely to be transmitted to the prison community (Ellenbogen 2009).

The Canadian prison system maintains family programs that allow inmates to have family visits every two months that may last up to 72 hours. These visits occur in separate units that are specifically designed for inmates and their families to have some level of privacy and autonomy. Some determining factors for inmate eligibility include inmates not being housed in a high security unit and not being at risk of committing family violence (Stern 2002). Additionally the Canadian prison system routinely conducts assessments to allow for early release of prisoners (Mauer 2006a), which likely contributes to lower prison populations and less overcrowding.

England and Wales

In England and Wales, overcrowding in the prison system has become a serious problem (Cavadino and Dignan 2006), with a prison population totaling 83,392 (which is a rate of about 153 per 100,000 people) (Walmsley 2009). An increase in the prison population has also been accompanied by an increase in the probation population (Comparative Imagination 2011). In the latter part of the twentieth century, a fear of crime dominated public beliefs (Kruttschnitt and Dirkzwager 2011). Although the crime rate itself did not substantially change, the growth in the prison population in the last few decades can be attributed to a shift to a more conservative political regime, combined with an increase in the amount of media attention focused on crime (Newburn 2007, as cited in Kruttschnitt and Dirkzwager 2011). In 1975, the prison population was 39,820, a rate of 81 per 100,000 people (Cavadino and Dignan 2006). This means that the prison population has more than doubled in recent decades, and the rate of incarceration has almost doubled in just over 35 years. Due to the increase in the prison population, most inmates are housed two to a cell (Kruttschnitt and Dirkzwager 2011). Unlike in the United States, where an inmate to officer ratio of 100:1 is not uncommon, in the U.K. the ratio of 10:1 is more commonly found (Edgar and Martin 2000, Wood 2006, Byrne and Hummer 2008). Racial disparity exists in the prison system, with minorities comprising only 9 percent of the general population, but representing 23 percent of the prison population (Cavadino and Dignan 2006).

Similar to the United States, the increase in the prison population is in part due to harsher sentences. The Crime Sentences Act of 1997 increased the sentence length for repeat offenders. Three major tenets of this act include 1) a life sentence on conviction of a second offense that is either violent or sexual, 2) a mandatory minimum of seven years for the third conviction of Class A drug trafficking, and 3) a mandatory minimum three-year sentence for those convicted of their third burglary conviction (Newburn 2007, as cited in Kruttschnitt and Dirkzwager 2011). Additionally, under the Criminal Justice Act of 2003, some violent and sexual offenders are also subjected to an indeterminate sentence in the interest of "public protection" (Kruttschnitt and Dirkzwager 2011). A great number of inmates are incarcerated for offenses that include violent offenses, drug related offenses and burglary (Simon and De Waal 2009).

Although prior research has indicated that violence among prisoners in the United Kingdom is somewhat rare (Fitzgerald and Sim 1982), one of the most frequent violent offenses to occur is fighting, which is the classification generally used when there is a mutual assault with no clear victim or perpetrator. When examining the trends over time, the greatest number of incidents classified as fighting in prison located in England and Wales occurred in 1993 and 1994, with rates of 104 and 103 incidents per 1,000 inmates, respectively. The general trends prior to and after these two years show rates that range from 89 to 95 (Statistics of offences, as cited in Bottoms 1999). Assaults are also frequently reported among inmates. Based on victimization reports, 19 percent of inmates reported being assaulted, and 26 percent reported being threatened in the prior month alone (O'Donnell and Edgar 1998).

When compared with the United States, sexual violence appears to be less of an issue (McGurk, Ford and Barnes 2000, as cited in Sattar 2004). In their often-cited study on prison violence, Edgar, O'Donnell and Martin (2003) indicate that inmates in the United Kingdom are highly unlikely to be sexually victimized, a phenomenon that is comparatively more frequent in the United States. More than three-quarters of their sample had never been exposed to any type of sexual victimization, as a victim, assailant or witness. The infrequency of the occurrence is illustrated by a lack of prison slang to refer to sexual violence. Although argot exists for other common terms, such as homosexuals, the mentally ill and sex offenders, there are no informal terms used to illustrate prison sex.

The most violent of all offenses, homicide, is also the least frequent to occur, both in the community and in the prison system. Over an 11-year period, prisons in England and Wales experienced a total of 26 homicides, ranging from zero to five per year. During this same time period, the average prison population in England and Wales averaged 41,800 (Sattar 2004).

Unlike in the United States, very little research has been conducted which focuses on prison gangs. A major difference that has been cited is that, while prison gangs in the U.S. are almost exclusively based on race and ethnicity, those in England are more likely to form based on region (Wood 2006). Newly emerging research also indicates that gangs of Black Muslims have formed (Phillips 2012). There is an important distinction between gang activity between prisoners in the U.K. and the U.S. Whereas gangs in the United States often focus on violence, those in the U.K. seem to focus primarily on friendship and social networking (Phillips 2012).

The recent movement in the U.K. has been toward reducing opportunities for family visitation (Stern 2002). This may be due to concerns over safety for the family members, or due to logistical issues associated with the number of inmates. Regardless of the reason, this change could ultimately lead to an increase in prison violence for reasons discussed in subsequent chapters.

Scotland

Although the actual number of prisoners in Scotland is less than that of England and Wales (7,893) the rate is approximately the same, with about 152 prisoners per 100,000 people (Walmsley 2009). Scotland currently has 15 active prisons. Similar to the populations incarcerated in England and Wales, the offenses that are the most frequently sanctioned with imprisonment include violent offenses, drug offenses and burglary (Simon and De Waal 2009).

Until the 1990s, violence perpetrated by inmates against both fellow inmates and staff was relatively frequent (Wozniak 1989, as cited in Cooke, Wozniak and Johnstone 2008). Recently, there has been a decline in the levels of violence, especially serious assaults (Cooke et al. 2008). This decline has been partially attributed to making programs available to both inmates and corrections staff on reducing the frequency of violence (Walrath 2001, as cited in Cooke et al. 2008). Prisons in Scotland are also routinely inspected and assessed and the results of these assessments are provided to the public (Fairweather 2002).

Australia and New Zealand

Both Australia and New Zealand are beginning to take a more serious and punitive stance toward punishment (Cavadino and Dignan 2006). Australia has wide variations in their prescribed punishments. When compared with other nations, it has relatively large numbers of incarcerated individuals (Brown 1998, as cited in Cavadino and Dignan 2006), with a rate of 129 per 100,000 people (or a total of 27,615 people) (Walmsley 2009). Many of those incarcerated have been convicted of drug offenses, robbery or assault (Simon and De Waal 2009).

There are also striking differences in the demographics of those who are imprisoned. Just as the United States has large discrepancies between the White American populations and the African-American population, there is a vast overrepresentation of Aborigines in the prison system. Although those of Aboriginal or Torres Strait Island descent comprise a mere 2 percent of the total Australian population, they comprise a striking 20 percent of the prison population (Brown 1998, Freiberg 2001, as cited in Cavadino and Dignan 2006). Furthermore, because there is no federal system in Australia, each of the individual six states handles crime control differently. New South Wales, Queensland and West Australia experience high crimes rates. In contrast, Victoria, South Australia and Tasmania have comparatively lower crime rates (Cavadino and Dignan 2006).

Australian prisons are rife with violence and riots (Simon and De Waal 2009). The number of prison homicides per year averaged about three per year between 1980 and 1998, with an increase after 1994 (Dalton 1999, as cited in Sattar 2004). Homicides comprised approximately 7.25 percent of all deaths in custody. Sexual violence, on the other hand, tends to be less pronounced. Although many inmates report feeling fearful of sexual assault prior to their incarceration, most of the sexual activities that occur are reported to be consensual and not in exchange for promises of protection (Richters et al. 2012).

New Zealand has no federal system, but they also do not have separate jurisdictions. They only have one maximum-security prison, and about two thirds of their prisons are considered minimum security. Overcrowding is not a major concern for New Zealand, as most inmates are housed in single-celled units (Cavadino and Dignan 2006). New Zealand has a relatively large imprisonment rate of 185 per 100,000 people (Walmsley 2009), which has seen an increase in recent years. Unlike the United States, this increase is primarily a result of an increase in those who are committing serious crimes, especially violent crimes (Cavadino and Dignan 2006). It also is attributed to an increase in the punitive stance taken by politicians (Pratt and Clark 2005).

Russia

Russia has the second highest rate of incarceration in the world, with a rate of 629 per 100,000 people. There are 891,738 individuals housed in Russian prisons (Walmsley 2009). Historically, the nation had high imprisonment rates and low crime rates, but coinciding with the regime change, the crime rate has recently increased (Comparative Imagination 2011). The prison population has decreased by approximately 120,000 individuals in the last few years, as Russian officials have been releasing inmates due to the cost, overcrowding and poor prison conditions (Mauer 2006a). In 2010, in an effort to reduce violence and exposure of minor offenders to more serious ones, administrators began segregating first time offenders from those who are recidivists (Parfitt 2010)

Prison conditions in Russia are very poor and overcrowded. Guards are armed with guns and dogs, indicating an adversarial relationship between correctional officers and inmates. The prison culture is marked with high levels of physical and sexual violence and poor medical care, with thousands of reported cases of HIV and tuberculosis. More than 90 percent of the inmate population suffers from some form of a health problem (Parfitt 2010). The living arrangements are typically dormitory style or fenced living quarters, housing as many as one hundred inmates per individual unit (Hagemann 2008). Although work opportunities are scarce for inmates (Hagemann 2008), prisoners receive at least one family visit annually. These visits typically last 72 hours and take place in a secure housing unit within the facility (Stern 2002).

South Africa

South Africa is very much a transitional society, as it transforms from an authoritarian regime to one that is considered more democratic (Cavadino and Dignan 2006, Gear 2007). The Black population of South Africa is more likely to experience severe punishments than the White population (Cavadino and Dignan 2006). There are more than 164,000 people incarcerated, at a rate of 335 people per 100,000 (Walmsley 2009). Increases in the prison population since 1999 are due to increases in the numbers of individuals who are unable to meet bail, as well as the imposition of mandatory minimum sentences (Cavadino and Dignan 2006). Most offenders serving time in a South African prison have been convicted of sexual assault, rape or some other form of violent crime (Simon and De Waal 2009). High levels of unemployment in South Africa also mean that financial hardship motivates many crimes (Essuon, Simmons, Stephens, Richter, Lindley and Braithwaite 2009).

As the numbers incarcerated in South African prisons increase, so does the concern over institutional violence. The problem in South Africa becomes more pronounced when considering the levels of gang involvement. Just as in the United States, gang structures dominate much of the prison culture, and acts such as physical and sexual violence are paramount to exerting control (Goyer and Gow 2001, Essuon et al. 2009). This issue becomes even more concerning, as most inmates in South Africa are housed in communal cells, providing ample opportunities for violence to be perpetrated (Muntingh 2009). The increases in the prison population mean than overcrowding has become a much more significant issue, with many prisons holding more than double than the intended numbers (Goyer and Gow 2001, Van Zyl Smit 2004, as cited in Cavadino and Dignan, 2006; Simon and De Waal 2009). As many as 70 inmates may live in cells originally designed for 18 people (Goyer and Gow 2001).

Sexual assault has become particularly problematic among the prison population, with some estimating that as many as 70 to 80 percent of arrestees experience prison rape (Simon and De Waal 2009). Because South African culture is one that is stereotypically homophobic (Joint Working Group 2005), male on male rape has become closely associated with homosexuality (Gear 2007). In 2005, it was recommended that consensual sex among inmates not be considered a punishable offense (Anirudha 2005, as cited in Gear 2007). In South Africa (as is the case in some other nations), sexual assault is very narrowly defined as an act that involves forced vaginal penetration, limiting it to male on female interactions (Gear 2007). The goal of the revised policy in South African prisons may be to prevent punishment for traditionally taboo acts. However, as has been the case in other nations, correctional officers may have a difficult time discerning consensual sexual activities from those that are forced. This possibility, especially when coupled with the lack of reporting of sexual violence, may lead to fewer sanctions against those who perpetrate forceful sexual acts.

The prison population in South Africa, like other countries, is one that is subjected to selective enforcement (Thomas and Moerings 1994, as cited in Goyer and Gow 2001). As such, those who are incarcerated are also those who are the most at risk to be infected with HIV and AIDS: young, poor, illiterate, black males (Goyer and Gow 2001). Because there are no mandatory testing requirements for inmates, there is no official statistic on the number of HIV- and AIDS-infected inmates in South Africa. It has been estimated that as many as 60 percent of the incarcerated population is infected (Goyer 2002, 2003, as cited in Essuon et al. 2009). The spread of this infectious disease is of particular concern in South Africa, which currently has the largest number of HIV and AIDS infected people in the community. Many of those who have already contracted the disease are incarcerated, and engage in physical and sexual violence, as well as other behaviors including tattooing (Neser and Pretorius 1993, as cited in Goyer and Gow 2001), which further exposes the prison population to HIV and AIDS (Campbell 1997, as cited in Essuon et al. 2009).

Germany

Many offenders incarcerated in German prisons are violent offenders, although drug related offenses and theft are also commonly sentenced crimes (Simon and De Waal 2009). Although Germany once had one of the highest rates of imprisonment, the current rate is about 89 per 100,000 residents (or a total of 73,203) (Walmsley 2009). Relatively high prison rates were seen until 1983, primarily due to increases in sentences for violent and drug related offenses (Albrecht 1997, Feest and Weber 1998, Weigend 1997, as cited in Cavadino and Dignan 2006). The decreases seen between 1983 and 1991 were a result of less reliance on incarceration, from both prosecutors and judges (Cavadino and Dignan 2006), leading to a decrease in prison construction (Feest 1998, as cited in Cavadino and Dignan 2006). As prosecutors and judges return to their reliance on incapacitation as a primary mechanism of crime control (Cavadino and Dignan 2006), the prison population has begun to increase, though the numbers have not returned to the high numbers experienced in previous decades. This may be, in part, due to fewer prisoners being sentenced to shorter sentences. In Germany, "prison sentences shorter than six months are regarded as destructive and serving no penal purpose" (Tonry 2001: 4). Short sentences are seen as counterproductive, as they disrupt prosocial bonds, such as family and employment, as well as subject them to prisonization and stigmatization for life (Mauer 2006a).

A large number of those incarcerated in German prisons are "Russian Germans", which comprise between 8 and 14 percent of the total prison population (Federal Ministry of the Interior and Federal Ministry of Justice 2006, as cited in Zdun 2008). This Russian German population is often subjected to violence and coercion at the hands of other prisoners. For example, they may be forced to engage in sexually submissive activities, as well as clean the work stations and cells of other inmates, behaviors that are attempts to "feminize" them (Zdun 2008). The division between German prisoners and Russian German prisoners is one that mimics major gang divisions in some other nations.

Activities such as fighting, assault and smuggling drugs into prisons are relatively frequent (Zdun 2008). Although only about 9 percent indicate that they have been physically victimized, over 46 percent state they have been victims of psychological damage (Hagemann 2008).

The Netherlands

With a prison population rate of about 100 per 100,000 people (Walmsley 2009), the Netherlands once enjoyed an extremely low prison population. However, in recent years this has grown to be comparable to other European nations. Many believe that this increase is largely due to media exposure that emphasizes incapacitation as the primary mechanism by which to control crime. The idea of incarceration as the ultimate solution, as purported by American media, has not been historically accepted by the country. "The notion that the antidote to crime is to be tough on offenders is one that has largely infected the Netherlands from the outside, being foreign to the previous Dutch tradition" (Cavadino and Dignan 2006: 125).

The increase in the prison population can be blamed on both an increase in the level of crime, as well as a decrease in the public's tolerance of crime (Heiner 2005). In the past several years, the trend has been for the Dutch to be more punitive, and less geared toward rehabilitation and treatment (Boone and Moerings 2007, as cited in Kruttschnitt and Dirkzwager 2011), a trend that also mirrors that of the U.S. experience. Additionally, the increase in numbers may be misleading. Historically, if prisons did not have the necessary capacity to house new prisoners after they were found guilty, they were placed on waiting lists until room was available. Criticism over the waiting list, which had risen to 2,200 by 1990, has been cited to be the primary reason for the expansion of the prison system (Tak 2001).

A major difference between the Netherlands and the United States is that there is a distinct line drawn between the punishments meted out for serious crimes and non-serious crimes (Cavadino and Dignan 2006). Currently, the Netherlands employs four different types of prisons: remand prisons (for those awaiting sentencing), ordinary prisons, chronic offender prisons and detention facilities for illegal foreigners (Slotbloom et al. 2011).

Despite the increase in the prison population, the level of violence in Dutch prisons seems to remain relatively low. This may be due to majority of inmates being housed in their own cell for the bulk of their sentence (Tak 2001, Kruttschnitt and Dirkzwager 2011). Fights and assaults, considered frequent in many nations' prisons, are relatively infrequent. It is unclear whether this is due to a lack of prevalence or a lack of official reporting. As one prisoner puts it "You really have to struggle to be put on report" (Kruttschnitt and Dirkzwager 2011: 294). Moreover, prisoners are highly encouraged to participate in programming and regularly engage in labor to prevent assimilation of deviant criminal lifestyles (Tak 2001), which has been shown to prevent misconduct and violence.

Belgium

As of 2009, Belgium's prison population was 10,002, with a rate of 93 per 100,000 residents (Walmsley 2009). "Foreign prisoners" comprise approximately 40 percent of the prison population, which is loosely defined to include second or third generation immigrants, illegal aliens and international drug smugglers, among others (Snacken 2005).

Severe overcrowding and substandard living conditions have become issues in many Belgian prisons (Cavadino and Dignan 2006). The only rights that are guaranteed to prisoners include access to a lawyer and freedom of religion (Snacken 2005). Despite this, Belgian prisons seem to have relatively low levels of violence. The incidents that occur are generally related to decreases in work opportunities, feeling a lack of respect from correctional staff, and are most problematic in facilities that have the most severe overcrowding (Snacken 2005).

France

France's prison population hovers in the mid-range for Western European countries (Cavadino and Dignan 2006), with a population of 59,655 (a rate of about 96 per 100,000) (Walmsley 2009). A reasonably large number of prisoners residing in French prisons are considered foreigners, and many of these are there due to work permit violations (Gallo 1995, as cited in Cavadino and Dignan 2006). Inmates serving short sentences and those who are awaiting trial are housed in *maison d'arrêt* prisons. These prisons are considered the most overcrowded of the French prisons, operating at about 20 percent beyond their designed capacity (Dorozynski 2000). French prisons are primarily filled with offenders who have been found guilty of theft, rape, sexual assault and violent offenses (Simon and De Waal 2009).

The prison conditions in France have been noted as being unsanitary and overcrowded (Simon and De Waal 2009). The extent of the deplorable conditions was brought to the public's attention in 2000. As a physician in the French prison system, Veronique Vasseur (2000) accounts the results that overcrowding and poor living conditions can have on inmates. During her years at the La Santé Prison, she witnesses countless incidents of violence, including rape, suicide and self-mutilation, and she notes that cells were routinely infested with rate, mice and insects (Dorozynski 2000).

Unfortunately, very little research exists that focuses on sentencing and imprisonment in France. Even research examining crime and crime rates is scarce. Monetary issues and bureaucratic structures seem to be at the heart of this issue, causing many to blame "the fragmentation of funding" for the lack of information (de Maillard and Roche 2004: 144). Relying on anecdotal information, such as that provided by Vasseur, would suggest that the conditions of French prisons would lead to relatively high rates of violence among inmates.

Italy

Italian laws stress rehabilitation over retributive based punishments (Cavadino and Dignan 2006). The country's rate of incarceration is relatively low in comparison with other European countries. Since the 1980s, the Italian government has made strides to attempt to reducethe country's prison population, which is currently 55,027 (with a rate of 92 per 100,000). Some efforts include increased use of fines, "semi-liberty" prisoners (who spend at least ten hours per day in prison), and special leave for some prisoners (Cavadino and Dignan 2006). Once an individual has been accused of a crime, they are not permitted to plead guilty to a lesser offense in an attempt to reduce their sentence (Simon and De Waal 2009).

Approximately half of the incarcerated population consists of prisoners are on remand (Cavadino and Dignan 2006). The convicted inmate population is primarily comprised of those found guilty of either violent or drug related crimes (Simon and De Waal 2009). Many of those incarcerated are illegal immigrants who cannot take advantage of the lengthy trial process, which includes two appeals (Nelken 2011).

The overcrowded conditions are forcing Italian prisons to no longer accommodate inmates in single celled units. Despite this, there seems to be little concern expressed over individual violence. As is typical, inmates express concern over inappropriate and overcrowded prison conditions (Cavadino and Dignan 2006). Aside from this and the very occasional escape, there have been few violent incidents reported in Italian prisons.

Sweden and Finland

Both Sweden and Finland use incarceration sparingly. When compared with other nations of Northern Europe, these countries have relatively low incarceration rates. Sweden's incarceration rate is 74 (6,770 prisoners) and Finland's is 64 (3,370 prisoners) (Walmsley 2009). Between 1976 and 1992, the incarceration rate declined approximately 40 percent after concern over the increasing prison population lead to policies such as increasing the use of suspended sentences (Mauer 2006a). The offenses individuals are most likely to be incarcerated for include violent and property crimes, as well as drunken driving (Simon and De Waal 2009).

In comparison with other nations, prison conditions are relatively good in these two countries. Although about one-third of prisoners indicate being psychologically abused, physical violence is substantially less frequently cited. About 8 percent of Swedish prisoners and less than 4 percent of Finnish prisoners report being physically victimized (Hagemann 2008).

Both conjugal and private visits are allowed. Prisons maintain apartments in close proximity so that inmates can spend quiet time with their family members (Stern 2002). Prisoners also continue to be allowed to take advantage of community resources, such as medical care and social services (Stern 2002). It seems that prisoners in Sweden and Finland are less removed than prisoners that reside in other countries, which likely contributes to lower rates of violence.

Israel

The nation of Israel operates 24 prisons that house 22,788 inmates, representing a rate of about 326 per 100,000 people (Walmsley 2009). Israel's incarceration rate is most closely approximate to that of South Africa. Although the incarceration rate of the nation trails that of the United States and Russia, it has a much higher rate than most countries, including New Zealand, Scotland, Australia, England and Wales. Violent crimes are the crimes most frequently associated with incarceration in Israel, but burglary and sexual offenses are also relatively common (Simon and De Waal 2009). There are also a large number of Palestinians being held as political prisoners, as will be discussed in Chapter 4.

Some Israeli prisons have basic educational opportunities, vocational training and opportunities for employment while incarcerated. Inmates who are housed in lower security level facilities also have opportunities for visitation, which are limited in frequency to one per month (Simon and De Waal 2009). Furlough and parole opportunities are also available. Inmates must serve at least two-thirds of their prescribed sentence to be eligible for parole (Simon and De Waal 2009).

There is a lack of information available on the prison climate in terms of violence. One form of violence that has been examined among Israeli prisoners is sexual violence. Sexual offenses, including harassment and rape, infrequently occur and are negatively viewed by inmates (Einat 2009). Those who perpetrate sexual offenses are viewed as "mentally and physically weak and thus contemptible" (Einat 2009: 659). This is in sharp contrast to the views of many prisoners of Western nations, who generally view sexual aggression as an avenue to obtain and maintain power and masculinity over other inmates.

Einat (2009) speculates on the differences between the prison cultures and posits three primary explanations. First, the spread of HIV and AIDS among the Israeli population has generated fear and concern over unsafe sexual activities. Also, the community population of Israel is less likely to engage in violence than many Western nations. As such it may be that those entering the prison system are less likely to have underlying violent tendencies that result in engaging in violence while incarcerated. Finally, the overwhelming majority of prisoners housed in Israeli facilities are affiliated with religions that denounce sexual assault (predominately Muslim and Jewish faiths). Therefore, they may be more likely to fundamentally oppose sexual assault than those who belong to other religions or who have no religious affiliation.

China

China's incarceration rate is 119 per 100,000 people, equaling 1,565,771 people. This numbers excludes the approximately 850,000 individuals being detained in administrative detention (Walmsley 2009). China's incarceration rate falls in between the rates of Australia and Canada. The staff to inmate ratio is approximately 1:5.6 (Simon and De Waal 2009).

Prisoners are distributed among 679 correctional institutions (Simon and De Waal 2009). Under the decentralized institutional system, various classification policies were used in determining the security level of the facilities to which the inmates were sent. In recent years, there has been an effort to move the facilities away from remote areas and toward more centralized locations in order to ease management of the facilities and to encourage more frequent family visitations. This movement is also accompanied with a new classification system that mimics other nations. This includes categorizing inmates to maximum-, medium- or low-security facilities, primarily according to the type of offense and the length of the prison sentence (China to classify prisoners).

Chinese prisoners are granted visitation, though the frequency is limited to family members, and to no more than two visits per month. Visitors are expected to bring items such as toiletries, bedding and towels for the inmates (Simon and De Waal 2009). Seriously ill inmates are granted parole in order to have access to the appropriate medical treatment, and other inmates who display "outstanding behavior" are also given the opportunity to be paroled (Simon and De Waal 2009: 107).

The prison conditions in China seem to be shrouded in secrecy, leading to speculation and potentially "fictitious rumors" that "distort the facts" (Mingdi).

The nation's prisons seem to encounter similar issues as other countries, including occasional violence from correctional officers and poor living conditions in some facilities (Mingdi). Assumedly, crowding would contribute to prison violence, as is the case in other nations, though the more conservative nature of the Chinese culture may contribute to violence being infrequently perpetrated among the inmate population.

Japan

Japan's rate of incarceration is low, at 63, with 81,255 individuals residing in prison (Walmsley 2009). The low rates of both crime and imprisonment are attributed to Japan's unique culture. Many lesser offenses are handled informally and outside of the purview of the criminal justice system. The most frequently cited offenses among those incarcerated in Japan include larceny/theft, assault, fraud and robbery (Simon and De Waal 2009). Reintegrative shaming is commonly used to deal with offenders (Braithwaite 1989), and informal social control mechanisms are generally sufficient to deter crime, as well as control those who have committed crime (Time 2012).

Despite a low rate of incarceration, there has been an increase in Japan's prison population. According to the Annual Report of Statistics on Correction, the number of inmates increased from less than 40,000 in 1992, to approximately 65,000 in 2005. This increase is illustrative of major revisions to the Penal Code in 2004, including an increase in the maximum sentence length for commission of a single offense from 15 years to 20 years (Hamai and Ellis 2008).

The increase in the prison population has coincided with an increase in public punitiveness towards offenders. A culture once renowned for its reintegrative shaming and restorative justice policies is exhibiting a marked shift in its attitudes. Although Japan still enjoys a relatively low crime rate, it is slightly increasing. This, coupled with a few high profile and egregious crimes has prompted the Japanese public to show less of a forgiving attitude toward offenders. However, when former inmates reoffend, the blame is generally not placed on the offender, but on the correctional service. Japanese society expects parole to properly monitor the inmates upon their release, and expects the institutions to provide rehabilitation and treatment services while they are incarcerated (Hamai and Ellis 2008). Correctional facilities believe that "rehabilitation is based on remorse" (Geraci 2003: 87). All inmates are provided with education, and drug abuse prevention, vocational training and religious services are readily available (Geraci 2003).

Some populations have disproportionately increased. Both the numbers of mentally ill and aging offenders have risen substantially (Hamai and Ellis 2008). For instance, the number of inmates that are age 60 and over increased 87 percent between 2000 and 2006, while in the community there was only a 17 percent increase in this age bracket increase during this time frame (Onishi 2008). In order to deal with the unique health and mobility issues this aging population presents, the Justice Ministry built specially designated units within the prison to house older inmates (Onishi 2008).

Even the most minor prison infractions are documented and punished. The range of potential punishments divvied out to the inmates range from verbal warnings, to reductions in food rations, to solitary confinement (Simon and De Waal 2009). Although the rates and types of prison infractions are not readily available for Japanese prisons, it seems logical to assume that the combination of rehabilitation programs and opportunities, combined with a low tolerance for behavioral infractions, would lead to lower levels of serious violent incidents.

Conclusion

Although the United States has the highest incarceration rate worldwide, Russia follows closely behind. In comparison with the other countries included in this discussion, these rates are approximately two to seven times greater. Some of these countries have lower crime rates than the United States. In many cases, however, these discrepancies exist as an artifact of differences in sentencing policies. Longitudinally, individual countries have experienced increases in their prison populations when they adopt "tough on crime" stances, as can be seen with the Netherlands.

It should be noted that the punitiveness of a country cannot be measured by the prison population alone. For instance, Germany is a country that is likely to avoid handing down shorter sentences to avoid the negative effects of prison among those who commit minor offenses. In contrast, other countries, such as Finland, are likely to dole out shorter sentences to offenders (Nelken 2011). Which of these two sentencing philosophies is the least punitive? Other factors aside from incarceration rates, such as the reliance on intermediate sanctions, sentence length and general climate of the prison system are vital components to understanding how punitive a nation may be.

Prison violence is a relatively new topic of interest, and some nations are hesitant to openly allow research in correctional institutions. Because of this, the literature on prison violence from an international perspective is relatively scarce. One theme that seems to emerge is that more crowding equates to more opportunities for violence in an environment where supervision of inmates becomes more difficult to achieve. Examples of this are clearly portrayed by the United States, Russia and South Africa, the nations with the three largest per capita imprisonment rates. Prison misconduct and violence also seem to be less problematic when programs exist to keep inmates occupied and focused on community reintegration.

Chapter 4

Prison Violence: Explanations and Theoretical Underpinnings

Introduction

Before examining the potential consequences and solutions for combating prison violence, it seems intuitive that the possible reasons for the occurrence of this violence should be explored. Some theories focus specifically on explaining the prison violence phenomenon, such as the importation and deprivation theories. Explanations of inmate behaviors are almost always rooted in discussions of the prison hierarchy and the convict code. Although less frequently applied in the literature, more general criminological theories are also applicable to exploring possible causes of violence among inmates.

The Process of Prisonization

Inmates live in an environment that is far different than in the free community. Over time, inmates often assimilate into a world of violence and fear, where norms, values and beliefs counter those that people in the general population find acceptable. This process has been termed prisonization (Clemmer 1940). The process of prisonization occurs as inmates adjust to the unique nature of the behaviors of their fellow inmates. As individuals become more assimilated into the prison culture, they have more difficulty reintegrating into the community upon their release.

One example that shows how acceptable behavior differs from that in society can be seen by looking at disorderly conduct. Disorderly conduct, including engaging in violence against other inmates and correctional staff, may be used as a form of expression among inmates when they are dissatisfied with the way they are being treated (Crawley and Crawley 2008).

Individuals do not all experience prisonization in the same way, or to the same degree. The length of time incarcerated, as well as the total amount of time spent behind bars throughout a lifetime, can dramatically alter an individual's degree of prisonization. The experiences while incarcerated can also have significant effects. For example, inmates who maintain prosocial ties with the free community (such as with noncriminal peers and family members), or those who achieve an education or participate in programs, may feel more closely tied to the outside world. They may be less likely to fully adopt the antisocial values that are rampant in an institutional setting.

Wheeler's (1961) U-curve thesis provides an interesting insight to addressing prisonization. This theory states that inmates exhibit the most prosocial behavior at the beginning and at the end of their prison sentences, and are the most prisonized at the median point of their sentence. For example, during the first six months of a sentence, the newly admitted inmate is likely adjusting to being away from their family, friends and community. They then begin to adopt the attitudes and behaviors of the other inmates. Six months prior to their release, they will prepare for their release by actively engaging in treatment and other prosocial programming to ease their transition back into the community. As more inmates are sentenced to longer prison terms, they spend longer periods of time in the horseshoe portion of the U-curve, indicating they may have more difficulty shedding their prisonized personas.

The Prison Hierarchy

The prison hierarchy would suggest that there is a "pecking order" among inmates. The likelihood of an individual being either the perpetrator or the victim of a violent offense may be partially determined by his or her place on the prison hierarchy. There have been many different versions of the prison hierarchy discussed in the literature, but the earliest and most well known is the hierarchical structure proposed by Gresham Sykes (1958).

At the top of the prison hierarchy are those who actively engage in aggressive masculine roles. Known as "wolves", this group engages in assault to prove their masculinity and avoid being victimized by other inmates (Sykes 1958). Various forms of violence may be perpetrated by those considered "wolves", including threats of violence, as well as both physical and sexual violence. Through their aggressive physical and sexual behavior, they avoid being labeled as a homosexual. Ironically, commission of sexual violence is a means to exert their masculinity and dominance over other inmates. Sexual behavior that is more consensual however, is often considered emasculating to members of this group (Man and Cronan 2001).

Another tier of the hierarchy is comprised of inmates who fulfill typically feminine roles, such as washing laundry, cleaning other inmates' cells or growing their hair long. They are highly unlikely to perpetrate violence against other inmates. They are likely to adopt more passive or submissive roles. This group, which is primarily comprised of individuals who are either dispositionally or situationally homosexual, is thought to be adapting to the prison environment (Man and Cronan 2001).

"Punks", in contrast, are typically coerced into sex with wolves, often through physical force (Sykes 1958). Because they are often physically weak and unable to defend themselves, they are prime victimization targets for the stronger members of the hierarchy (Man and Cronan 2001) and may even be traded or used as commodities by wolves (Sykes 1958). The inmates who are the most notoriously victimized by other inmates are those who committed sexual offenses against a child (Faulkner and Faulkner 2006).

The prison environment becomes a hierarchical system among inmates, as they attempt to exercise informal social control over one another, primarily through various forms of physical violence (Hensley, Wright, Tewksbury and Castle 2003). For example, the sexual assault committed against same-sex members of the prison community mirrors the heterosexual rape that occurs in the free community, as aggressors seek out other inmates to rape in an attempt to sexually exploit and "feminize" them (Donaldson 2001, Donaldson 2003, O'Donnell 2004). Also, as in heterosexual rape, the act is not usually about sex, but is more about the power and violence the aggressor associates with the rape (Dumond 2000).

Inmates are able to advance to the higher stages of the hierarchy by exerting dominance over other inmates. Minor infractions against one's masculinity, such as threats of violence or theft of personal property, may be met with physical violence. Physical violence may been seen as the best, if not the only, way to protect physical possessions, or protect their nonmaterial interests, such as loyalty, respect and honor (Edgar, O'Donnell and Martin 2003, Hassine 2010). It is important to note that the violence does not have to be acted upon. Simply the threat of violence is often enough to maintain control over other inmates (Bordieu 2001, as cited in Trammell 2011).

One of the issues with much of the research is the way in which the individual's place in the hierarchy is viewed. Certain assumptions are made, such as that an individual's race, age, involvement in gangs and length of their sentence all determine their placement in the hierarchy. It is also understood that these roles are not stagnant, as an inmate's placement may vary over time and space (Sykes 1958). However, the ease to which these transformations occur is relatively unclear. Joining a gang and committing violent acts are well-documented mechanisms by which to advance in the hierarchy. Conversely, not protecting oneself from an attack reduces an inmate's credibility and likely their pecking order in the prison hierarchy.

The Convict Code

The subculture of inmates is one that places emphasis on ideals such as toughness and individuality, while at the same time recognizing that inmates should show loyalty to each other, rather than to correctional staff. As expressed by Sykes (1958), the original tenets of the convict code include for inmates not to snitch on each other, to show loyalty to other inmates (and not to correctional staff), and not to show any signs of weakness. As the nature of prisons and their populations have evolved over time, additions such as loyalty to an inmate's racial group and reliance on violence have also emerged.

While some doubt the existence of the convict code altogether, others argue that the code may have evolved over time or may even vary based on the individual institutional values. For example, when discussing his personal experiences at Graterford Prison, Victor Hassine states that the underground economy guides the norms and values of the inmates. The unwritten tenets of the code include inmates excluding certain behaviors from their routines, such as gambling, becoming involved with homosexual activity, stealing, borrowing or lending property, and being involved with drugs (Hassine 2010). All of these behaviors discussed by Hassine have been linked with violence (Porporino et al. 1987, Sattar 2004, Hochstetler and DeLisi 2005, Edgar 2008), perhaps signaling a trend in inmate populations to intentionally avoid violence. Furthermore, inmate relationships may not be as cohesive as they once were. One example is the change in how snitching is perceived. Although it is still condemned, it is generally a more tolerated behavior than in previous years (Faulkner and Faulkner 2006).

It may be the changing nature of the prison population. As those who are considered true "convicts" begin to disappear, they are replaced with those who may not have been imprisoned in decades past. As discussed elsewhere, particular populations such as the mentally ill and street gang members have begun to dominate the U.S. prison population (Terry 2003, Hassine 2010). As such, the values that once dictated the behaviors of the inmates have also evolved, leading some to believe that the changes in levels of violence may be due to prisons more closely mirroring street life rather than traditional prison life (Hunt, Riegel, Morales and Waldorf 1993, as cited in Terry 2003). It may also be that as prisons become more crowded, inmates may be more self-serving than in the past. As more people compete for scarce resources, such as work or educational opportunities, inmates may be less likely to adhere to the convict code, which is meant to bind them together.

If a true convict code, as described in previous years, does not truly exist, there may be some question as to why such a myth may persist. Keeping a belief in the code alive is ultimately beneficial to inmates because they may see it as a way to prevent being victimized. As new inmates arrive, they will be less likely to attempt violence against those who are already prisonized. For correctional staff, it may provide justification for inhumane treatment toward inmates (Hassine 2010). If inmates are perceived as violent and virtually uncontrollable populations, it may be easier to excuse and receive support for physical force that may otherwise be viewed as excessive.

Importation Versus Deprivation Theory

Are inmates likely to offend against one another because they are predisposed to crime? Or is it the torture of imprisonment and the loss of freedom that leads them to commit offenses while incarcerated? Criminologists have been speculating on answers to similar questions for decades.

The importation theory suggests that those who are incarcerated are criminogenic to begin with. Specifically, there are characteristics of the individuals behind bars that make them qualitatively different than the law-abiding population (Irwin and Cressey 1962). These individuals may be suffering from drug addiction, may have been raised in a criminogenic neighborhood, or myriad other explanations. Regardless of the reasons, they are predisposed to committing offenses, and it follows that they may continue to commit crime, even while incarcerated. Importation theorists would also support the belief that prisons serve as "schools of crime", where offenders can not only improve on the techniques associated with their current offense, but also perhaps learn techniques associated with committing new types of crimes.

Contrast this with deprivation theory, which states that it is institutional life, not the individuals that comprise the institution, which leads to continued crimes behind bars (Sykes 1958). Prison is meant to be a "total institution" (Goffman 1961), one which controls absolutely, gives all inmates similar statuses, and provides all basic needs for the inmates. A consequence of complete confinement is known as the pains of imprisonment. As described by Sykes (1958) these pains include loss of security, autonomy, liberty, access to goods and services, and heterosexual relationships. The loss of these mainstays of human life lead to frustration, anguish, and, eventually, to committing crime.

Since the inception of these two models, others have introduced theories incorporate ideas from these, as well as other aspects of prison life. The coping model states that it is an individual's failure to cope with prison life and its demands that leads to offending (Toch 1977). The situational model explains that it is the nexus of the "who" (as stated in the importation model), with the "where" (as stated in the deprivation model), combined with whom else they are incarcerated with (Steinke 1991, Jiang and Fischer-Giorlando 2002).

The Informal Economy

There is no question that the informal economy that is created inside prisons is an explanation for some of the violence that occurs in the facility. In part due to a lack of ability to participate in a legitimate market, inmates often participate in an informal black-market system. This system consists of physical goods, including weapons, drugs and cigarettes. Services, such as housekeeping duties, protection from violence and sexual favors, are also traded in this system. Quinn (2003) notes three primary characteristics of the informal inmate economy: 1) items, such as cigarettes, are used as currency, 2) almost all inmate transactions violate institutional rules and 3) violence is relied upon for dispute resolution.

Weapons are a high priced commodity. Despite the attempts made by facilities to prevent the existence of weapons, as will be discussed in Chapter 7, their existence continues to pose problems. Weapons can be made from items commonly found in the institution, including toothbrushes, magazines and metal pipes. Visitors or correctional staff can also smuggle them in. Weapons pose obvious threats to the safety of inmates, correctional staff and visitors. Because of the potential for serious injuries and fatalities caused by weaponry, although correctional staff may ignore other black-market transactions, they are considerably less likely to do so in the case of weapons (Kappeler and Potter 2005).

Because a large number of inmates are identified as substance abusers, drugs also play a significant role in the black market. Drugs also enter the prison economy through visitors and correctional staff, and essentially any drug available outside the prison walls will find its way inside the facility, including marijuana, cocaine, crack and heroin. Drugs in the institution have drastically inflated prices. Drugs typically are sold for between three and four times as much as they would on the street (Crewe 2005). Since inmates do not have access to the amount of cash needed to purchase these drugs while they are incarcerated, money is typically exchanged between buyer and seller representatives on the outside (Seiter 2011). Due to the high risk and inflated costs, and because the drug market is primarily controlled by organized gangs, nonpayment results in serious violence (Seiter 2011).

In the absence of cash, cigarettes are a main source of currency in prison. Prisons have varying policies on cigarettes, with some banning them altogether. Lankenau (2001) examined the effects of these bans and found that they include increased prices, increased demand and increased levels of violence. Moreover, the effects of smoking can be even more harmful if prisons enforce these bans. If inmates are unable to have cigarettes smuggled in from the outside, they are more likely to make their own. They often resort to rolling cigarettes in pages from Bibles, which are known to be printed with toxic ink (Lankenau 2001).

Anything not specifically permitted in a correctional facility is considered contraband. Once an item is labeled as contraband, it is likely to become a commodity and increase in value on the black market. The link between this informal economy and violence is logical and is seen in the community as well. As demand increases, supply decreases, and cost subsequently increases. The difference is that inmates do not have access to legitimate means of obtaining money, and thus rely on either outside financial sources or barter other goods and services in order to participate in the black market. If they are unable to do so, then they are likely to be violently victimized by their debtors.

The Female Prison Experience

Female prisons differ from male prisons in the general interactions among the inmates. Females generally view violence as an unnecessary tool of informal control (Trammell 2012). Instead, they form small communities or families, called pseudo-families, as a mechanism to cope with the isolation of prison life (Ward and Kassebaum 1965, Keys 2002). Approximately 70 percent of female inmates rely on pseudo-families to become more acclimated to the prison culture (MacKenzie, Robinson and Campbell 1989, Trammell 2012). Unlike male prisons, there may be fewer attempts to dominate the other inmates, and physical violence is relatively infrequent among female inmates (Irwin and Owen 2005). Violence is reserved for situations where they feel it is truly justified, such as when they feel wronged by another inmate, rather than as a means of dispute resolution. They are also more likely to disrupt a fight or assault in progress than male inmates (Edgar, O'Donnell and Martin 2003), indicating that levels of informal social control among females are relatively great.

This may be, in part, due to women being more likely to be nonviolent offenders than males (Chesney-Lind 2002). Therefore, hierarchical structures are considered unnecessary, as female prisoners organize themselves into communities that mimic familial structures (Giallombardo 1966, Hefferman 1972, Foster 1975, Keys 2002). These families mimic the familial structures found in the free community, and are generally comprised of a mother, father and siblings. Female inmates see these as positive mechanisms to help with their adjustment to prison (Trammell 2009). It may be these pseudo-families that lead to many women reporting that they actually feel safer in prison than they did when they resided in the community (Bradley and Davino 2002).

Unlike male inmates, females are unlikely to join gangs. For males, race is an important factor in male prisons, leading to both formal and informal segregation among the inmate populations. Gangs are the primary mechanism for informal socialization, and race is the determining factor for gang membership. Women are more likely to create bonds based on personal experiences, such as the struggles associated with leaving their children while they are incarcerated (Trammell 2012).

There remains some question as to whether female inmates are less likely to engage in violence or if there are other factors that complicate the matter. Women may be less likely to report victimization, or their victimization may occur at the hands of correctional officers and staff. Their victimization may be more likely to take other forms, such as coercive victimization. Although prior research would indicate that violence rates among females is significantly lower than male inmates, recent research indicates otherwise. For instance, when examining physical violence rates, Wolff, Blitz, Shi, Siegel and Bachman (2007) found that annual female rates of victimization are 92 per 1,000 inmates, compared with 75 per 1,000 male inmates. When examining violence rates across the entire period of incarceration, males had higher rates of victimization than females (252 in comparison with 204 per 1,000), but these numbers indicate female victimization rates that are much greater than traditionally believed.

Although women may be less likely to engage in violence and other prison misconduct, they are treated differently than their male counterparts. They are far more likely to be officially sanctioned for breaking the rules, even for minor infractions (Dobash, Dobash and Gutteridge 1986). Females, for example, are frequently cited for swearing and yelling; both of these behaviors are commonplace in male facilities and generally not sanctioned (Trammell 2012).

Women are also more likely than men to engage in what may be termed emotionally assaultive behavior, such as verbal threats, attempting to break up relationships or spreading rumors (Irwin and Owen 2005, Trammell 2009). Female inmates may see this type of behavior as more damaging than physical violence. As one inmate illustrates, "Women will fight with words; these words hurt more than the fist" (Trammell 2009: 277). Known as relational aggression, this type of psychological and emotional violence is "used to ruin relationships and sever social ties" (Trammell 2012: 101). Considering the prominent role that inmate relationships play in helping these females become acclimated to the prison culture, the damage from emotional and psychological abuse cannot be overemphasized. Females who are victimized in these ways will likely have difficulty integrating into the larger prison culture, as well as into individual pseudo-families, ultimately becoming ostracized from their fellow inmates. Inmates with no social ties to one another may be more likely to suffer from psychological issues.

Many women report issues such as depression, post-traumatic stress symptoms and suicidal thoughts (Slotbloom et al. 2011). These issues appear to be similar to psychological issues reported by male inmates. However, women are far more likely to have endured abuse than their male counterparts. Prior to their incarceration, females are highly likely to have been abused emotionally, physically and/or sexually (Green, Miranda, Daroowalla and Siddique 2005, Blackburn, Mullings and Marquart 2008). In fact, it is often the avenues by which they attempt to escape violence in the community that result in their initial incarceration, such as prostitution and substance abuse (Bradley and Davino 2002).

Deprivation factors appear to be more prominent for female inmates than importation factors (Slotbloom et al. 2011). For example, women report missing the associations and contacts with their family members, especially their children, while incarcerated (Richie 2002). Fueling the lack of contact with family members is the long geographical distance that female inmates' families in particular must travel, with an average of 160 miles (Richie 2002, Travis 2008).

Early studies of sexual activity in women's prisons focused on consensual sexual relations among inmates. The sexual roles adopted by the inmates are paramount to understanding sexual activities. Those who become labeled as "butch", the more dominant role, surrender much of their femininity in exchange for power and control. The "femme" inmates, in contrast, provide the butch prisoners with nonsexual services or goods in exchange for sexual favors (Ward and Kassebaum 1965). While homosexuality has become more accepted among prisoners of both genders, it has gained even greater acceptance among female prisoners in comparison to males (Hensley 2000). Moreover, sexual activity among female inmates may be viewed as womanly and seductive, even by the victims themselves (Banbury 2004). Therefore, it may be that homosexual acts behind bars have gained a wider acceptance, irrespective of whether such acts are consensual or forced. Targets of sexual assault may be less likely to perceive themselves as victims if they do not consider the act as criminal, and therefore less likely to report it.

It has also been posited that rates of female sexual assault may actually be higher than those of males. Female prisoners are qualitatively different than male prisoners and are subjected to more formal social control, equating to a more accurate portrayal of official assault statistics than is obtained from male prisons (DeLisi 2003). Correctional officers of female facilities may also believe that females need more emotional support (Struckman-Johnson, Struckman-Johnson, Rucker, Bumby and Donaldson 1996), and therefore be more involved in the day to day activities of individual prisoners. This means that sexual offenses may be more likely to be detected among females than males.

Another possibility for a higher rate of sexual victimization for females is the lack of females in the inmate population as a whole. Because there are so few female inmates, they are often misclassified and placed into prisons that are not at the appropriate security level (Easteal 2001). Classification systems designed for male inmates are likely to "over classify" female inmates, placing them in more secure facilities than is needed (Van Voorhis and Presser 2001). The implications for female over classification can be profound: crowding and higher security levels are both positively correlated with violence among female inmates (Steiner and Woolredge 2009). Assigning an inmate to an institution that has a higher than necessary security level may lead to that individual being victimized by the other potentially more violent inmates. In contrast, placing a female prisoner in a facility with a less than adequate security level may lead to that individual reacting violently and taking advantage of the other members of the inmate population.

Although women are often revered as being less violent than men, either as a function of either socialization or biological differences, they may be at least as likely to engage in sexually violent behavior, though it may not be as overt as violence expressed by males (Underwood, Galen and Paquette 2001). Earlier research found that females might be equally as susceptible to express sexual violence as their male counterparts, especially during their menstrual cycle (Ellis and Austin 1971). There are a few potential explanations for this correlation. It may be that a system of rewards and punishments is less important during their cycle as they potentially suffer from depression and mood swings. It also could be a process of social learning, in which female inmates believe they can get away with more while suffering the symptoms associated with premenstrual syndrome (Ellis and Austin 1971).

Many female inmates report incidents of staff-perpetrated sexual assault (Easteal 2001, Irwin and Owen 2005), with approximately half of the total number of sexual assault incidents being initiated by correctional officers and staff (Struckman-Johnson and Struckman-Johnson 2002). Some evidence points to "rings" of correctional officers, loosely organized within prisons, engaging in coercive sex with inmates. These rings can consist of as many as half of the officers on staff (Day 1998). Such encounters may potentially be more stressful and traumatizing than those instigated by other members of the inmate population, especially if the officer is male. Assault by a male correctional officer has the potential to be more physically violent and result in more serious injuries than those perpetrated by fellow female inmates. There is also a risk of the female inmates being impregnated by the offenders, resulting in children being born to a mother who is unable to care for them due to her inmate status.

This issue was highlighted by a Human Rights Watch report in 1996, which stated that male correctional officers were sexually assaulting female inmates. The government, the public and academia quickly became interested in this controversial topic (Hensley, Struckman-Johnson and Eigenberg 2000). In 1999, the United State General Accounting Office published a special report addressing this high profile issue. Over the three-year span of this special study, 506 reports of staff on inmate assault were filed, though only 18 percent of the allegations were sustained (Women in Prison 1999).

The factors that contribute to staff perpetrated sexual abuse of the inmates are quite different than those involving inmate-perpetrated abuse. The initial relationship between offender and victim is vastly different than the relationship between inmates, especially since the outcomes of an inmate's prison experiences are directly related to their relationships with correctional officers (Easteal 2001), and the power differential between the two parties. Female inmates, who are often referred to as "girls" by staff members, experience a parent–child-type relationship with correctional officers (Easteal 2001). Because of the power imbalance, many women in prison believe they have little to no control over the events occurring in their lives (Collica 2002).

Correctional officers have extreme amounts of direct authority over the inmates they supervise and have the ability to use their own discretion when determining the appropriate measures to take in disciplining them. They have the authority to use physical force and punishment, with inmates often having little recourse for inappropriate displays of power (Calhoun and Coleman 2002, Pogrebin and Dodge 2001). As such, it is often expected that the officers may step beyond the bounds of reason and use levels of force that are not only unnecessary, but are also inappropriate. Extreme amounts of force are often easily justified by the officer, and outcries from the inmates often become a matter of credibility between the inmate and the officer (Pogrebin and Dodge 2001).

The general routines of the prison environment also reflect policies that allow the opportunity for such acts to occur. Often sexual violations may be camouflaged as drug searches or other forms of "pat and strip" searches (Easteal 2001, Calhoun and Coleman 2002, Banbury 2004). Although they have become part of the routine in female prisons, many inmates view these as another form of sexual misconduct perpetrated against them by correctional staff (McCulloch and George 2009). Inmates often report strip searches as humiliating and degrading experiences, as well as unnecessarily enforced. Women may feel uncomfortable with certain officers conducting these searches, but the level of comfort is less a matter of the gender of the officer than their inappropriate behavior during the search (Calhoun and Coleman 2002). However, prisons continue to use such measures to ensure safety and to prevent paraphernalia from entering the facility, and refusal of strip searches may result in a loss of privileges, such as visitation rights (McCulloch and George 2009), which are often of utmost importance for female inmates.

Similar to inmate perpetrated incidents, semi-consensual relationships and coerced sex between staff and inmates seem to be more common than overt sexual assault. Inmates may use sexuality as a commodity and trade sexual favors for privileges, such as visitation rights, phone calls and other amenities (Calhoun and Coleman 2002, Pogrebin and Dodge 2001). Inmates may also voluntarily engage in consensual sexual activities or even romantic relationships with one or more correctional officers. This is in part due to the differential treatment that female inmates receive in comparison to males. By considering the emotional state of females, staff and inmates are placed in a position in which the professional distance between the two parties is diminished (Calhoun and Coleman 2002). However, since the power imbalance between staff members and inmates is so extreme, even seemingly consensual relations are dominated by an overwhelming feeling of powerlessness on the part of the inmates (Calhoun and Coleman 2002).

General Criminological Theories

As stated earlier, there is surprisingly little research that incorporates general criminological theories into explanations of violence among inmate populations. Prisons are communities with unique characteristics, norms and values providing a population on which to explore theoretical explanations. Many theories, including deterrence, routine activities, social bond, techniques of neutralization, anomie/ strain, subculture, learning and labeling theories can be applied to gain a greater understanding of prison violence.

Deterrence Theory

In 1764, when Cesare Beccaria wrote *Of Crimes and Punishments*, he illustrated the primary concepts of deterrence theory. Although deterrence is now often used as a justification for harsh punishments, originally Beccaria wrote his theory in order to condemn excessive punishments, including torture and capital punishment. Deterrence can be broken down into two basic types: specific and general. Specific means that after an individual is punished for wrongdoing, they will not want to commit offenses again, for fear of experiencing a similar punishment. General deterrence states that when an individual commits an offense, and they are punished, others will be deterred from committing offenses for fear of being given a similar punishment. Deterrence theory assumes that offenders are rational actors who weigh the costs and benefits prior to committing a crime. Both specific and general deterrence theories rest on the assumption that the punishments 1) occur swiftly after the offense has been committed, 2) have a degree of certainty of being exacted and 3) are severe enough to be seen as an adequate punishment. In addition to these principles, in order for general deterrence to be effective, punishments must also be made known to the public.

When referencing deterrence theory within a correctional context, the punishment prescribed could be those meted out by the correctional administration for infractions pertaining to violence. Punishments for breaking the rules in prison range from verbal warning to being placed in solitary confinement. Lesser punishments, such as warnings, are generally reserved for minor rule breaking, and more severe punishments are doled out for violent misconduct. While solitary confinement is certainly seen as a severe punishment among inmates, and generally occurs relatively swiftly after the offense has occurred, the certainty may be called into question. Inmates are not inclined to report violent victimizations committed against them, as will be discussed in Chapter 6. General deterrence may therefore not be achieved through institutional punishments. Moreover, specific deterrence is also likely not achieved. As expressed by some inmates who fail to officially report being victimized, the ultimate fear is based on the likelihood of retaliation upon the offender's return from solitary confinement to the general population. An individual who continues to commit offenses, even after being sanctioned, has certainly not experienced specific deterrence. Moreover, because most violence is spontaneous, most assailants are not afforded the appropriate time to engage in the cost–benefit analyses that are necessary for deterrence theory to be feasible (Ross 2008).

Deterrence theory may also be viewed with the inmates themselves exercising punishment over one another. In particular, potential inmate based punishments, such as violence, may carry more weight in deterring crime than official punishments given by the administration. This phenomenon is seen particularly within correctional institutions that have high levels of violence or threats of violence. The individual experiences of the inmate determine their level of fear (Woolredge 1998), and inmates are more likely to feel fearful in an environment that perpetuates violence. Feeling safe is a basic human need, and inmates often respond by exhibiting toughness in an effort to prevent being victimized (Edgar, O'Donnell and Martin 2003).

Routine Activities Theory

Routine activities theory follows a similar principle of deterrence theory by stating that the offenders are rational actors. This theory posits that crime is an opportunistic event. Individuals commit offenses when they believe they are the least likely to be caught, and when the potential rewards are the greatest. According to this theory, in order for a crime to occur, there must be 1) a suitable target, 2) a motivated offender and 3) an absence of capable guardians (Cohen and Felson 1979, Felson 2009).

This theory clearly can be applied to prison violence. In prison, there is no shortage of either suitable targets or motivated offenders. Prior research has posited that those who are the most likely offenders tend to be African-American (Hensley, Koscheski and Tewksbury 2003, Hensley, Tewksbury and Castle 2003, Austin, Fabelo, Gunter and McGinnis 2006), those who have been incarcerated longer (Sykes and Messinger 1960, Dumond 2000, Man and Cronan 2001), those who have a history of violence, especially gang-related violence (Man and Cronan 2001, Cunningham and Sorenson 2007, Drury and DeLisi 2011), those who are larger in stature (Dumond 2000), and those who are not classified as older (over 50) or younger (in their early 20s) (Man and Cronan 2001, Hensley, Tewksbury and Castle 2003). It can also be explained on an offense level. Those who have been shown to be the most at-risk to commit violent offenses behind bars include those convicted of robbery, kidnapping, carjacking and assault (Sorenson and Davis 2011). In contrast, those who are the most at risk of being victimized, the suitable targets, are those who are white, newly incarcerated, nonviolent offenders, smaller in stature, and younger than the average 29-year-old inmate (Man and Cronan 2001, Banbury 2004, Cunningham and Sorenson 2007). Individuals who have committed the most violent offense in the community, homicide, are the least likely to commit violence while they are incarcerated (Sorenson and Davis 2011).

The crucial component for routine activities to be useful in preventing violence among prisoners seems to be the presence or absence of capable guardians. Correctional officers and other staff comprise an obvious example of capable guardians (Sechrest 1991). Of course, the staff to inmate ratio should be considered. Not having enough correctional officers to effectively manage the prison population is endemic to violence, and many prison wardens believe that increasing the supervision of the inmates will decrease the amount of violence among the inmate population (Moster and Jeglic 2009). The attitudes of the correctional officers who are present are also important. If the guardians are nonchalant, unresponsive, poorly trained or poorly paid, they may do little to prevent violence, especially violence that is relatively minor such as threats, simple assaults or nonviolent coercive sexual acts (Money and Bohmer 1980, Struckman-Johnson and Struckman-Johnson 2000, Tartaro 2002).

The presence of other inmates, who could either promote or prevent a violent incident, can also be included in this population. Fellow inmates may serve as capable guardians and prevent potential violence. This is particularly relevant when considering the group mentality that is often endemic to the prison culture. An inmate who considers exacting violence against another inmate may be thwarted from doing so if there is a potential threat of retaliation by other inmates. Gang membership is illustrative of how some inmates may be prevented from becoming violent against their rivals. Furthermore, the existence of surveillance cameras may also be considered a capable guardian. Many prisons have installed CCTV systems to fulfill guardianship, in addition to correctional officer presence. The effectiveness of CCTV systems is discussed in more detail in Chapter 7.

Different areas within the prison may be more likely to locations for violence to occur. Areas where guards are less likely to be present, such as inmate cells, are the most likely sites for violence (Lockwood 1980, Lockwood 1982, Wright and Goodstein 1989, Tartaro 2002, Hensley, Wright, Tewksbury and Castle 2003, Banbury 2004, Sattar 2004, Austin et al. 2006). Focusing specifically on sexual assault, inmates are the most likely to report feeling either very unsafe or unsafe in the showers (32.09 percent), their own cells (21.97 percent), the dormitory area (21.74 percent), the gym (21.35 percent) and the day room (19.63 percent) (Levan-Miller, 2007). These locations are those at which correctional officers may be less likely to be present, or which have unstructured activities, in comparison with areas where there may be more structure and more supervision. For example, educational facilities and work areas have been found to be less frequent locations for violence (Atlas 1983a, Steinke 1991).

Social Bond Theory

Social bond theory tries to explain why people do not commit crime. When individuals are more closely tied to conventional norms and institutions, they are less likely to engage in criminal activities. There are four major bonds, as described by Travis Hirschi (1969). Attachment refers to our attachment with other people, such as family members, peers or community members. An individual's commitment to their stake in society can also prevent them from committing crime. Commitment generally refers to the status a person has achieved as a result of their employment or educational endeavors. Involvement in noncriminogenic activities, such as education or recreation, may be seen as a means to prevent crime. Finally, maintaining similar beliefs as the societal norm is thought to serve as a barrier to offending. Believing that mainstream society does not condone crime means individuals are more likely to conform to society's norms.

Prisoners are far removed from mainstream society. Contact with loved ones is limited, and visitation is often difficult for family members. Many may have difficulty finding transportation to facilities that are geographically distant from their communities (Sabbath and Cowles 1992, Petersilia 2003). Contact with others is limited to what the institution provides. Other services such as education, counseling and religious programming, create a financial and logistical burden to facilities.

According to social bond theory, maintaining these bonds is crucial in preventing offending. Inmates who are able to be educated, engage in employment and maintain contact with their families while incarcerated may be less likely to engage in violence against other inmates. It may indeed be the lack of employment and other opportunities that create idleness among prisoners, giving them ample time to commit violence against one another (Hassine 2010).

Techniques of Neutralization and Drift Theory

Techniques of neutralization and drift theory posit that people "drift" between law-abiding and criminogenic behaviors. An individual does not consistently commit crime. Someone with a stable job and home life may also engage in criminal activity. Neutralizing criminal behaviors becomes essential to some people as a means to justify their wrongdoing. Sykes and Matza (1957) provide examples of neutralizing behavior, including condemning the condemners, appealing to higher loyalties, denial of the victim, denial of injury and denial of responsibility. It is believed that using these techniques may assist offenders in psychologically dismissing and justifying their criminal behaviors.

Inmates find themselves in an environment behind bars that is drastically different than mainstream society. The acceptance of violence as an appropriate means of dispute resolution provides an ideal backdrop for justifying behavior. The "us versus them" mentality inmates feel toward correctional officers, as well as to members belonging to rival gangs or other racial or ethnic groups, may allow inmates to justify violence against these individuals. If inmates do not view violence as inappropriate, it seems they may be likely to not condemn these actions, either as perpetrated by themselves or other inmates, particularly if an inmate engages in an activity that is seen as appropriate and necessary. For example, an inmate owing gambling debts or refusing sexual advances from a more powerful inmate may be viewed as infractions that, from an inmate's perspective, warrant physical or sexual violence (Levan-Miller 2008).

Anomie and Strain Theories

Anomie literally means "without laws", or a condition of normlessness. Developed in the 1940s, Merton's anomie/strain theory builds on Durkheim's idea of anomie. According to Durkheim, people may begin to feel anomic when their society experiences rapid change (1893). During times of rapid societal change, people struggle to find their niche in society. Durkheim explained that suicide, for instance, occurs during times of both economic depression and economic prosperity, as people are either unable to achieve their set goals or are unable to ascertain their own limitations (1897).

Merton's revision describes a disjuncture between life's goals and means. Goals are measures of success, often based on financial achievements, such as material possessions. The means are the avenues by which individuals strive to achieve these goals, usually through educational and employment opportunities. The crux of Merton's theory is in describing how individuals adapt to the availability of goals and means (Merton 1942).

Anomie theory seems particularly relevant considering the isolation of prisoners from the free society. As prescribed by Durkheim, inmates are likely to feel both alienation and purposelessness, in part because they have little to no contact with the outside world. Furthermore, they may feel a lack of goal commitment, especially if the institution is not designed to provide education or employment training opportunities. Early prison research alludes to anomic prison conditions via the pains of imprisonment (Sykes 1958). As such, violence may be partially explained by anomie theory, in that inmates are committing offenses against one another because the anomic conditions of the institution are not providing them with a "normal" societal structure.

Similarly, strain theory may help explain particular aspects of the prison culture that make sexual assault more likely among inmates than among other populations. The conditions of confinement are more likely to encourage negative stimuli and to remove positive stimuli, making the achievement of individual goals difficult. The characteristics of individual prisoners, such as race, age and the length of their sentence, in accordance with their individual values can help determine whether the strains caused by imprisonment will result in misconduct, such as violence (Blevins, Listwan, Cullen and Johnson 2010). If we are to assume that physical dominance is a commonly aspired to goal, then it is understandable that inmates would feel a compulsion to achieve that goal, regardless of the means to obtain it. In terms of sexual dominance, among a same-sex population, it is therefore a natural occurrence that sexual aggressiveness and dominance are an attempt to adhere to a "normal" structure, where the victims may be representative of the female element in the free society.

Subculture Theory

The belief that some subcultures within society have different norms and values than mainstream society is the focus of subcultural theories of crime. Some theorists have purported that the high levels of crime and violence among some lower-income populations may be due to those populations holding different ideals as positive (Wolfgang and Ferracuti 1967). A "lower-class culture" is one that maintains different norms and values than mainstream culture. According to Miller (1958), members of the lower class are likely to place an emphasis on 1) trouble, 2) toughness, 3) smartness, 4) excitement, 5) fate and 6) autonomy.

Subculture theories have been more recently revised to discuss the "code of the streets" (Anderson 2000, as cited in Cheeseman 2003). When feeling alienated from mainstream society and culture, individuals may turn to violence as a way to survive and prove their masculinities. Respect becomes the primary form of currency, and feeling disrespected by others gives license to retaliate, sometimes violently, against those transgressors (Brookman, Copes and Hochstetler 2011).

These theories seem particularly relevant to inmates, as they subscribe to primarily deviant and violent values and attitudes. The prison subculture is one that rewards violence, and with a lack of punishment given to inmates combined with peer approval of such activities, the violence becomes justified within the confines of the prison walls (Toch 1985, as cited in Cheeseman 2003). Similar to the patterns of a lower-income neighborhood, it is seen that crime and violence are ways of life for offenders, both in the community and behind bars. While incarcerated, inmates are expected to adhere to the convict code, which is comprised of distinct norms, values and behaviors that often counter those which exist in general society (Sykes 1958, Dumond 2000). Having a large group of individuals who follow patterns of norms and attitudes which contradict those of conventional society (though are not necessarily homogenous with one another) lends itself to criminality. Moreover, if inmates are housed in prisons in which they view the conditions as poor or unlivable, they may view correctional staff as adversarial (Biere 2011).

Paralleling the lower-class culture thesis, Cheeseman (2003) argues that inmates value:

- Trouble – By getting into trouble and engaging in violence, inmates are exerting control over one another. Using violence as a form of trouble can be a means to gain contraband and other goods and services (Bowker 1983, Toch 1985).
- Toughness – Masculinity and domination is demonstrated by inmates in the form of toughness. Even as illustrated by the convict code, weakness is not a trait that is acceptable among inmates.
- Smartness – Just as in Miller's original tenets, smartness does not refer to formal education, but rather a reliance on "street smarts". For inmates, these street smarts are pronounced by outsmarting correctional staff (Allen and Bosta 1981, Cheeseman, Mullings and Marquart 2001), as well as proving their intellectual prowess over other inmates by using these street smarts combined with violence (Bowker 1983).
- Excitement – Risky behaviors, such as violence, sex, gambling, drugs and smuggling contraband, are rampant in prisons. Because prison activities are routinized and monotonous, these behaviors are often welcome by inmates to create excitement in an otherwise structured lifestyle. Indeed, this creates a particular problem for correctional administrators, as activities, such as fighting and other forms of violence, create more of a benefit to the inmates by creating excitement, making them more difficult to thwart (Toch 1985, Page 2002).
- Autonomy – Autonomy is a commodity that inmates do not generally have, as all their actions are dictated by institutional schedules and rules. Frustration with a lack of autonomy often results in violence, either against other inmates or correctional staff (Bowker 1980, Light 1991).
- Fate – The fatalistic viewpoint that inmates feel is reflected by how they believe correctional staff may view them (Baskin, Sommers and Steadman 1991, Montgomery and Crews 1998). Inmates may feel that if they are being seen as dangerous and inhuman, then their behavior is either beyond their control or is justified against those who are their oppressors.

Learning Theory

Learning theory posits that individuals who are exposed to particular types of behaviors are more likely to mimic those behaviors. At its most basic level as an explanation of crime, learning theory would hypothesize that those who are the most likely to engage in crime are those who are exposed to it, through their families, friends or communities. Individuals may couple this exposure with having the motives, rationalizations and drives to see law-abiding behaviors as unfavorable. Furthermore, a propensity to commit crime is based on the frequency, duration, priority and intensity of the exposure to the criminal behavior (Sutherland 1939).

The process of rewards and punishments for various behaviors also condition individuals to either engage in or avoid particular behaviors (Skinner 1938).

Many of the inmates serving time likely began committing crime as a result of being exposed to crime while they were living in the community. Residing in facilities where there are others residing who view crime and violence favorably is an obvious breeding ground for more crime and violence. Although institutions have punishments in place for violent infractions, inmates may not consider these as important as the rewards they could potentially reap from their fellow inmates. Inmates gain a sense of empowerment from exerting violence over their fellow inmates, which they likely view as a significant reward for their violent actions. In terms of the frequency, duration, priority and intensity of exposure, institutions that house large numbers of highly violent inmates are likely exposing a multitude of inmates to violence, which will likely result in transmission of those violent values onto other inmates.

Labeling Theory

Labeling theory suggests that there is a self-fulfilling prophecy involved in crime commission. Individuals commit crime because others believe them to be criminogenic and have labeled them as offenders. A person's master status, or their primary role, becomes a criminal one, and all other roles diminish in comparison. Although some version of labeling theory has existed for a century, Lemert (1951) is often credited as being the primary theorist for labeling theory. Lemert explains that labeling theory only applies to secondary deviance, and it cannot be used to explain primary deviance. Primary deviance is the criminal act that takes place before the label has been applied. Secondary deviance refers to the criminal acts that occur after an individual has been labeled as a result of their primary deviance. Becker (1963) would later explain that it is the label that is attached to the act and the actor that is problematic; the consequences of the act are often less harmful than they are labeled.

Inmates label each other based on their offenses and on their behaviors while incarcerated. Those who are more violent and actively involved in a gang are more likely to commit violence against inmates that they have labeled as weaker. Those who have committed sex offenses against children, in contrast, are labeled by other inmates and specifically targeted for violence. Furthermore, correctional staff and administrators label offenders upon intake as part of their classification process. Inmates are generally assigned to housing based on their offense. They also further label and sanction them based on their behaviors while incarcerated.

Violence in Extraordinary Circumstances

Both a prison-specific theoretical basis and a more generalized criminological theoretical basis can be used to explain incidents of prison violence that become routinized to the daily prison regime. Some forms of prison violence, however, are considered rare or extraordinary. A few examples of this type of violence include collective violence, prison escapes and enemy combatants who are held in detention facilities.

Collective Violence

Much of the violence that occurs is between individual inmates, or between small numbers of inmates, such as group or gang violence. Sometimes, prison violence can take a more collective form, such as disturbances or riots. Disturbances are considered less severe than full-scale riots, as they generally involve fewer inmates and often do not last as long, usually being disseminated relatively quickly by correctional staff. Riots, on the other hand, involve all or a majority of the inmate population, and can last hours or even days at a time. Although the number of riots per inmate reached epic proportions in the United States in the mid-1970s, they have decreased dramatically over the years, especially with the approach of the millennium (Useem and Piehl 2006).

Because of the duration and potential physical harm to inmates and correctional staff, riots can be highly publicized and often generate significant public attention to the prison system. Some of the infamous prison riots that have occurred worldwide in the last several decades include:

- Attica Correctional Facility, Attica, NY (1971) – 43 killed
- New Mexico State Penitentiary, Santa Fe County, NM (1980) – 33 killed, more than 200 injured
- Strangeways Prison, Manchester, England (1990) – 1 killed, 194 injured
- Carandiru Penitentiary, Sao Paulo, Brazil (1992) – 111 killed
- Iquique, Chile (2001) – 28 killed, approximately 150 injured
- El Porvenir Prison, Honduras (2003) – 86 killed

These incidents represent only a handful of collective violence incidents. As with most violent acts, riots, which are typically more serious and involve more fatalities than disturbances, are also more likely to receive significant media attention.

According to the American Correctional Association, riots may be attributed to several factors, including inhumane treatment, overcrowding, poor correctional management, inadequate correctional programming and idleness among the inmate population (Quinn 2003). Contrary to popular belief riots often do not spontaneously erupt, but are often a culmination of inmate dissatisfaction over time. As Carrabine (2005) explains, "riots are at the high end of disorder and, in crucial respects, a key task is explaining why a riot happens in one place, while at another, only a lesser disturbance occurs" (907).

There are two primary competing theories that have been applied specifically to prison riots. One is the inmate-balance theory, which states that as prison officials become more authoritarian, they reduce what little freedom and few privileges inmates have. This erosion of freedoms and privileges results in frustration and anger, sometimes leading to rioting. The second theory is called the administrative control theory. As a result of a weak, unstable or divided correctional management, inmate riots and disturbances are more likely to occur (Useem and Reisig 1999).

Like many violent incidents that occur in prison, collective violence can be explained by inadequate supervision, combined with a relative deprivation of relationships, programs or privileges. After a highly publicized riot occurred in California in 2009, Barry Krisberg, President of the National Council on Crime and Delinquency was quoted as responding, "if you isolate these men from their families and cut down even the most basic educational and counseling programs, you're going to create more idleness, and this is what happens" (Moore 2009).

Escapes

Prison escapes are extremely rare occurrences. When the infrequent escape does occur, however, it generally receives significant media attention, especially if the escapees are violent offenders. The national level data on prison escapes is not readily available to the public (Culp 2005), so much of what is known about escapes has been compiled by individual researchers.

It has been estimated that annually, about 1.4 percent of the correctional population escapes (Culp 2005). The reality of those few escapes is very different from the media portrayals of typical prison escapes. The majority of the escapes that occurred in 2002 (almost 87 percent of the total escapes) occurred among those who were in the community, participating in work release programs or furloughs (Camp 2003, as cited in Stinchcomb 2011). The few inmates who successfully complete a "true escape" from an institution are unlikely to resort to violence to complete their escape. Most who escape from institutions either cut or scale a fence or perimeter, with only a handful of escapees using physical force or violence against correctional staff (Culp 2005). (See Figure 4.1 for an example of an unusual prison escape.)

The number of total escapees has been declining in recent years. This may be due to an increase in correctional supervision, or it may be because there are comparatively few inmates who are completing work release programs or furloughs. It may also be based on the changing demographics of the prison population, as discussed in Chapter 2. Most escapees are young, White males who have committed property offenses (Culp 2005). While the reasoning behind this statistic is up for interpretation, as the correctional population shifts to primarily house young, African-American males who are incarcerated for commission of drug offenses, the rates of escapes have subsequently declined.

On December 13, 2000, seven inmates escaped from the John B. Connally Unit, located near Kenedy, Texas. The maximum security facility houses approximately 2,800 inmates. The seven men were all serving long sentences for severe crimes ranging from injury to a child to murder. They planned their escape during a particularly slow time of a time in the maintenance area, which had relatively low levels of surveillance. After knocking several individual unconscious (including maintenance workers, correctional officers, and other inmates), they stole their clothing and identification, stole weapons from a guard tower, and then stole a truck before fleeing the facility. They left behind a note that read, "You haven't heard the last of us yet".

After their escape, they committed two robberies and killed police officer Aubrey Hawkins when he attempted to apprehend them. On January 21, five of the men were found near an RV park in Colorado. Four were taken into custody and the fifth shot himself in the chest after a standoff with police. The last two men were captured two days later. The six men were taken into custody, and all were sentenced to death. To date, two have been executed, and the remaining escapees are residing on death row.

In many ways, this escape represents a very atypical one. The inmates were all serious offenders, serving time in a maximum security facility for serious crimes. Their escape was relatively elaborate and preplanned and involved action against correctional officers. They also committed additional violent offenses once they escaped from the facility, and were not captured until several weeks after their escape.

Figure 4.1   "The Texas Seven": an unusual prison escape

*Source*s: Hollandsworth 2001, Notorious Texas Seven 2008, Graczyk 2012

Political Prisoners

According to Amnesty International, political prisoners are those who are "held in prison or otherwise detained for their involvement in political activity and/or for their religious or political beliefs", or "who are deemed by a government to either challenge or threaten the authority of the state" (Simon and De Waal 2009: 125). Political prisoners are found in many countries, including Russia, China, Israel, Iran and the United States. Among the nations that house political prisoners, the United States maintains that it does not incarcerate people as political prisoners, and that all of those who are detained are criminals (Simon and De Waal 2009).

Individuals who are detained as political prisoners are quite different from those who reside in prisons designed to hold U.S. citizens. First, these individuals can be held indefinitely, even without being found guilty of a crime. They also are not provided with the rights afforded to individuals according to the stipulations of the Geneva Conventions. Because the detainees are tried in military tribunals rather than by a standard court, they are not guaranteed the same rights as United States citizens being tried on U.S. soil. For instance, rather than be tried by a jury of their peers, they are tried by a small group of military commissioners. The mere fact that the average citizen knows of the existence of these supposedly secret military prisons – such as Abu Ghraib, Diego Garcia and Guantanamo Bay – is indicative of the significance of the violence that occurs behind the walls of these institutions (Gordon 2009).

Perhaps one of the most controversial detention centers for military combatants is the one located in Guantanamo Bay, Cuba. Opened in 2002 at the beginning stages of the United States' "War on Terror", Guantanamo Bay is designed both as a military prison and an interrogation camp. Some controversial interrogation techniques that have reportedly been applied include subjection to extreme temperatures, sleep and food deprivation, punching, slapping and water boarding (Greenberger 2007). Interrogations are extreme, and it seems that while the original intention of the traditional prison is to reform the inmates, at Guantanamo Bay, "the ultimate goal is to transform the prisoner into a individual who is docile, obedient, and useful" for the purposes of interrogations (Welch 2009: 11).

While the form of resistance against formal control mechanisms in typical prisons often takes the form of gangs, inmate on inmate violence or inmate on staff violence, this is not necessarily the case at Guantanamo Bay. While there have been some issues with collective violence, the resistance often manifests into mass suicides or hunger strikes (Welch 2009). There is no readily available data on the prevalence of inmate on inmate violence; however, because the inmates are under such massive levels of scrutiny, it is expected that most violence could be prevented. Interpersonal violence would likely take control away from the guards and prevent furtherance of goals related to eliciting confessions and information form the detainees.

Justification for treating detainees as enemy combatants was originally based on extreme and emergency considerations. Secretary of Defense Donald Rumsfeld stated that Guantanamo Bay would be reserved for the worst of the worst and those who represent a true threat to national security. Despite this claim, the bulk of the detainees have been released, many with no charges pending against them, and returned to their countries (Greenberger 2007). Although there were previously around 600 detainees, as of March 2012, there are 171 detainees being housed at Guantanamo Bay.

The Obama administration has attempted to close Guantanamo Bay, citing opportunities for improved international relations as one benefit to its closure. Initially, the plan to close the facility included transferring the detainees to the existing supermax facilities in the United States. The majority of Americans, however, are not in favor of closure of the facility (Page 2009). Some oppose transferring the detainees from the facility to standard prison facilities for fear of recruiting existing inmates to fundamentalist groups (Spencer 2009). Perhaps the larger concern is that these individuals are not only being held without evidence of involvement in criminal activity, but are also routinely exposed to tortuous treatment.

The United States is certainly not alone in its confinement of political prisoners. Many nations opt to hold individuals for political purposes, and in many cases this also includes detainees or those who have not been found guilty of a crime. In Israel, almost all political prisoners are Palestinians. In 2008, there were an estimated 11,000 Palestinians in confinement (Palestinian prisoners 2008). About

60 percent of these political prisoners are being held for criminal charges, and the remaining 40 percent are being held on security charges (Simon and De Waal 2009). Questionable treatment surrounds their confinement as well. For instance, in 2005, visitation and phone calls were banned, making it impossible for these political prisoners to maintain ties with their families. Poor confinement conditions also continue to be an issue, including not being provided with timely or appropriate medical treatment, children being housed with adults, and some inmates being kept in solitary confinement for long periods of time (Simon and De Waal 2009).

As is often the case, extreme circumstances are often used to justify extreme punishments and consequences. Although there has been controversy and debate over the treatment of the detainees, much of this scrutiny has been on an international level. Despite the fact that all of the detainees have not been found guilty, nations remain divided on the treatment of the detainees, which is often based on the heinousness of accusations made against them.

Conclusion

The inmate subculture is complicated and very different from mainstream culture. Violence is not condemned, and is often revered among inmates. Research has typically focused on correction specific theories to explain prison violence. There is also a great deal of merit in applying more general criminological theories to explaining violence among correctional populations. Inmates are human beings, even if incarcerated, and the theories used to explain the criminogenic behavior that lead to their incarceration can also be used to explain their continued involvement in crime and violence while they are imprisoned.

Chapter 5
The Effects of Prison Violence

Introduction

Over 150 years ago, author Charles Dickens (1842) wrote, after visiting Eastern State Penitentiary, "It is my fixed opinion that those who have undergone this punishment, MUST pass into society again morally unhealthy and diseased". Conditions of confinement have greatly improved since Dickens' visit to prison. But, many of the effects on the individual inmate remain, leading to questions about the effects of the imprisonment experience.

The effects of incarceration are profound. Even if one is not directly violently victimized while incarcerated, being immersed in a world where violence is the norm, rather than the exception, can have devastating effects. Surprisingly, there is a lack of research on how exposure to violence while incarcerated may affect an individual's successful reintegration back into the community (Boxer, Middlemass and Delorenzo 2009). These effects influence the inmate, but also extend to the family, community and society as a whole.

Much has been written about how families and communities are affected by an individual's incarceration; this research will be briefly discussed in this chapter in order to provide a backdrop for the struggles encountered. There is, however, scant research on how prison violence affects families and communities (Byrne, Hummer and Stowell 2008). As such, it becomes necessary to draw on victimization research in general to remember that having the status of prisoner or ex-convict does not alter the fact that many individuals released from prison are also victims of violence themselves.

The Effects of Incarceration on the Individual

Upon their return to the community, ex-offenders have numerous obstacles to overcome for successful re-entry. Despite the fact that they have served their prescribed sentences, they continue to be labeled as an offender by society. Simply carrying the status of an ex-felon means a loss of many previously guaranteed rights and privileges. In many states, those who have been convicted of a felony lose the right to legally possess a firearm or the right to vote (Wacquant 2001, Petersilia 2003). Their ability to obtain a college education is also greatly reduced by their automatic ineligibility for Pell grants and other forms of government-based tuition assistance, such as exclusion of eligibility for student-work programs or loans for those convicted of a drug offense (Ross 2008). Many offenders were already disadvantaged educationally prior to incarceration, with less than 13 percent obtaining any college education (Harlow 2003). Because many offenders herald from economically disadvantaged communities, they are less likely to emphasize formal education. Finally, felons are often denied access to social-welfare programs, such as food stamps, welfare or the ability to live in government subsidized housing. Thus, former inmates are crippled on their potential road to recovery.

The rationale behind some of these policies is questionable. Denial of Second Amendment rights was originally intended to prevent violent offenders from having access to firearms. But, many felons are convicted of nonviolent offenses. Denial of access to financial assistance may be thought to make these services more available to those who are not offenders. But, wouldn't society be better served in offering services to ex-offenders so they will be more likely to desist from crime?

Immediately upon their release, some states provide "gate money" (averaging $69, but varying according to the state), while others only provide a bus or plane ticket home (Harrison and Schehr 2004). Once home they are expected to obtain and maintain stable employment to support themselves, a task that is often difficult (Henderson 2001, Cid 2009). Many states restrict the type of work a convicted felon may engage in, such as human resources, childcare or cosmetology (Rothstein 1999, as cited in Harrison and Schehr 2004). Additionally, they may be prohibited from handling money if they were convicted of a financial crime. These restrictions, coupled with the likelihood that the ex-offender does not have a stable employment history (in part due to their incarceration), make finding employment post-incarceration extremely difficult. Employers are also reluctant to hire someone who has been convicted of a crime, especially if that crime is a felony (Graffam, Shinkfield and Hardcastle 2008).

Taken together, these mechanisms by which society continues to exert control over offenders after they have been punished for their wrongdoing have the "sole purpose of accentuating the symbolic divide between criminals and 'law-abiding citizens'" (Wacquant 2001: 119). In short, being sanctioned for a criminal offense now makes these individuals qualitatively different from the rest of society, despite the fact that, at one time or another, many "law abiding" citizens have committed similar (or more serious) offenses. Ultimately, it is the contact with the criminal justice system, not necessarily their actions, that irrevocably changes the lives of these individuals. All of these mechanisms that are officially exacted by policies, however, pale in comparison to the emotional, mental and physical harm created by continuous exposure to violence. Despite the fact that violence has historically been an issue among prisoners, relatively few studies exist that examine the long-term issues associated with victimization (Jones and Pratt 2008).

The Effects of Violence on the Individual

Those who have been physically victimized most frequently report high levels of anger (Wolff and Shi 2009). Sexual assault victims are also likely to report anger, but also indicate high levels of depression, difficulty sleeping, persistent nightmares and general fear (Wolff and Shi 2009).

Simply feeling fearful of violence can have negative long-term psychological effects (Maitland and Sluder 1996, 1998, Lambert, Hogan, Barton and Stevenson 2007). Being fearful of other prisoners has been found to lead to stress, low levels of energy, depression and increased problems with physical health (McCorkle 1993). Exposure to violence often results in antisocial disorders (Boxer, Schappell, Middlemass and Mercado 2011), which may prevent former inmates from building the social bonds necessary to reintegrate into their communities. Those who suffer from antisocial disorders are less likely to seek out educational and employment opportunities, and may be hesitant to salvage family ties. Negative psychological effects such as those experienced as a result of fear can lead to increased levels of violence upon release (McCorkle 1993, Lambert et al. 2007). In essence, the experiences of prison are not easy to let go of, as illustrated by this passage:

> Abbott emerged from prison a celebrity, yet he remained dependent, no more than a child. Even in walking out of prison he did not "go free", because the prison was inside him. The minute he encountered pressure, he reacted with the fury and destructiveness cultivated in that prison. (Mason 1982: 564).

In the passage above, the author provides an apt description of prisoner and author of *In the Belly of the Beast*, Jack Abbott (Johnson 2006). Six weeks after Abbott's release from prison, he stabbed someone and was convicted of murder, which led to his return to prison. Twenty years after this incident occurred, he hung himself in his prison cell.

Mason could have been writing these thoughts about any prisoner, on any given day, being released from prison. Returning to the community, they cannot simply shed the prison experience from their mind. Whatever physical, sexual and emotional abuse they have encountered, either directly or indirectly, will surely follow them as they return to their previous lives on the outside. Although there has recently been significant research on the effects that sexual victimization may have on individuals, there is a lack of research on the effects of physical victimization (Boxer et al. 2009).

A great deal of research has been conducted on the effects of physical victimization among community members, especially youths. Among adult populations, being directly victimized or witnessing violence can result in symptoms such as anxiety, depression and aggression (Scarpa 2001, 2003, Scarpa, Fikretoglu, Bowser, Hurley, Pappert, Romero and Van Vorhees 2002, Boxer et al. 2009). These results have been replicated among inmates who either witnessed or directly experienced physical violence while incarcerated (Boxer et al. 2009).

Post-traumatic Stress Disorder (PTSD)

Post-traumatic stress disorder (PTSD) is a psychological condition that may occur after a particularly traumatic event. Violent victimizations, such as a sexual assault, physical assault or robbery, are prime examples of traumatic events. Other events that may lead to PTSD are those associated with feelings of fear, humiliation, guilt and helplessness (Johansen, Wahl, Eilertsen and Weisaeth 2007). All individuals who experience these events are not equally likely to suffer from PTSD. Some risk factors include continued exposure to violence, having a history of psychiatric disorders or having a history of previous victimizations. Groups who are at an increased risk of marginalization, such as women, ethnic minorities, those belonging to a lower socioeconomic status and the homeless are also at an increased risk of suffering from PTSD (Kelly, Merrill, Shumway, Alvidez and Boccellari 2010).

Considering the results of research that has been conducted on PTSD in the general community, this disorder seems particularly problematic among the inmate population (Grounds and Jamieson 2003). Inmates are likely victims of physical and sexual violence, but they are also individuals who must contend with the emotional struggles of prison life. The prison environment is one that creates feelings of fear (of violence), humiliation (though routinized activities, such as strip searches or a lack of privacy), guilt (or feelings of family abandonment), and helplessness (by being held captive). Many also have a history of psychiatric disorders, or have been exposed to violence, either in their communities or victims themselves. Moreover, we continue to incarcerate marginalized populations in greater numbers than ever before, including females, ethnic minorities, those of lower socioeconomic status and the homeless. We can therefore expect that prisoners who are violently victimized while they are incarcerated are at a significantly greater risk of experiencing PTSD, both while they remain in custody, and upon their release to the community.

Exposure to the violent nature of prisons is enough to cause life-trauma to inmates, regardless of whether or not they are the direct victims of violence. As one inmate states, "In the sense that life is cheap its treated cheaply in there…[of] all my experience in prison that's the one [I] hate the most and I don't know if I'll ever lose it" (Jamieson and Grounds 2005: 48).

Physical Damage

Physical injuries may result from both physical and sexual victimization. Victims of sexual assault are more likely to sustain injuries than those who are physically victimized (Wolff and Shi 2009). Many incidents require medical attention, and some even require hospitalization outside of the correctional facility (Wolff and Shi 2009). More than 1.5 million inmates have been released from prison or jail with a contagious or fatal disease (Gibbons and Katzenbach 2006). Victims of sexual assault are at risk of contracting a sexually transmitted disease, such as HIV, AIDS and Hepatitis (Knowles 1999, Banbury 2004). In the United States, infection of HIV and AIDS among the prison population may be as great as four to six times more prevalent than that in the general population (Hammett, Harmon and Maruschak 1999). Between 2006 and 2007, there were nearly 22,000 HIV and AIDS cases among state and federal inmates (Maruschak 2009). The greatest number of cases is among prisoners in the Southern states, with Florida and Texas contributing 3,626 and 2,450 cases, respectively. (See Table 5.1).

Table 5.1   Inmates in custody of state or federal prison and reported to be HIV positive or to have confirmed AIDS (2008)

Region	Number of inmates
Northeast	5.484
Midwest	1,814
South	11,003
West	2,148

Source: based on data drawn from Maruschak 2008
bjs.ojp.usdoj.gov/content/pub/pdf/hivp08.pdf

Part of the reason for the large number of HIV- and AIDS-infected individuals in prisons is because of the behaviors that inmates engage in that are considered risky. For instance, inmates are reasonably likely to use intravenous drugs, tattooing, and both consensual and forced sexual activity with other inmates and correctional staff. This problem is further exacerbated when considering that many of those in the community who have HIV will eventually be incarcerated, in part due to their participation in similar risky behaviors while living in the community.

One of the concerns associated with the large numbers of infected inmates include extreme health-care costs. Estimated health-care costs are more than $600,000 per AIDS- or HIV-infected inmate (Blumberg and Laster 2009). Keeping infected inmates in close quarters with other inmates who engage in risky behaviors also raises obvious concerns over additional contagion. However, once released, these inmates continue to bear the burden of their disease. Many do not have access to health care once they return to society, and may therefore receive no medical attention. They also now may infect family and community members with HIV or AIDS.

The Effects of Incarceration on the Family

As the prison population increases, so does the number of families affected by incarceration. Throughout the 1990s, the escalation was substantial, increasing from 1 million to 1.5 million children who resided in a home with an incarcerated parent (Travis 2008). The arrest and incarceration of a parent often has a profound effect on the children and the whole family unit, and these families are almost always marginalized by the larger community (Codd 2008). It has been argued that the results of having a parent incarcerated may be even more harmful than in the past because the average inmate is less likely to be the chronic and violent offender that was more commonly imprisoned in years past (Wakefield and Wildeman 2011). Moreover, because families that are the most likely to experience parental incarceration may already be troubled by other factors, such as poverty, it is believed that "incarceration has been pulling apart the most vulnerable families in our society" (Braman 2005: 123).

Forty percent of fathers resided with their dependent children immediately prior to their incarceration, and two-thirds of mothers were sole guardian for their dependent children (Travis, McBride and Solomon 2003). The ultimate residency of these children is dependent on which parent is incarcerated. In many cases, when a father is incarcerated, the child will reside with the mother or, is some cases, a relative. If the mother is incarcerated, the child often lives with a grandparent or other relative, often because the father is either incarcerated or is not involved with the child. Approximately 10 percent of children living with their mother are placed in foster care (Travis et al. 2003).

One result is less household income. Many make the assumption that the incarcerated individual would be more likely to either be unemployed or earn the bulk of their money through illegitimate means, such as theft or drug trafficking. On the contrary, 71 percent of those incarcerated in state prisons held legitimate employment immediately preceding their incarceration (Travis et al. 2003). Consequently, the spouses, cohabitants and dependent children of many inmates are left financially crippled. Many are left unable to support themselves. Some may move in with a relative or friend, and others become dependent on financial assistance through the government. Additional expenses may also be incurred by the family as a result of incarceration, such as additional childcare to compensate for the loss of a guardian and expenses in traveling to and from the correctional facility (Braman 2005).

Of course, finances are only part of the issue. The effects on the development of a child losing a parent can be devastating. Parent–child separation can result in impaired bonding, anxiety, antisocial behavior, acute traumatic stress, transmission of intergenerational crime and premature termination of the relationship with the parent. The latter two are especially pronounced among those who are aged 15 to 18 (Johnston 1995, Eddy and Reid 2002). These effects can begin to occur as early as infancy, and may become more pronounced as the time the parent is incarcerated increases. Of course, as more individuals are serving longer sentences than ever before, more children are at risk to experience more developmental effects than ever before.

The spouse or cohabitant that is left behind is also likely to suffer. In addition to financial burdens, they may experience stress from their concern of their loved one being in such a volatile environment (Braman 2005). They may also be stigmatized by their fellow community members for having a significant other who is incarcerated. Over time, this may lead to a resentment of the offender (Bilchik 2007). Many may choose to terminate their relationship altogether (Travis 2008).

Upon their return, many inmates report feeling distant from their children and spouse, and vice versa. Even those who have visitation with family members report, "communication and visits had been constrained and superficial" (Grounds and Jamieson 2003: 356). Limits on visitation and the lack of family-friendly visitation areas may prevent natural communication from occurring between prisoners and their loved ones. Returning home they often feel like strangers, as years have passed and they have missed major milestones in their lives. Furthermore, because the risk of divorce greatly increases with parental incarceration, returning inmates may be even further distanced from their families (Codd 2008).

The Effects of Violence on the Family

Although research has been culminating on the effects that prison violence has on the individual inmate, there is an absence of literature discussing the effects that violence may have on the family unit and the individual family members. Following the reasoning of cycle of violence theories, it is logically assumed that returning inmates suffering from depression, anxiety, anger, fear and PTSD would be more likely to engage in direct violence against their family members. It is expected that individuals exposed to prison violence would be more likely to engage in domestic violence upon their release.

Inmates suffering from sexual victimization would also carry negative consequences to their families. In addition to the above-mentioned consequences, sexual assault victims are also more likely to be infected with a sexually transmitted disease. For example, prisoners are more likely to contract HIV and AIDS as a result of a sexual assault or other activities while incarcerated. This means these diseases are also more likely to be transmitted to spouses, significant others, or anybody else who engages in sexual activity with them.

The end result of prison violence, in addition to the effects of incarceration on the family, is obvious psychological and physical damage. By subjecting individuals to violence behind bar, the criminal justice system may be condemning their family members to follow in their footsteps. For youths, this may mean the cycle of intergenerational crime and violence is doomed to be repeated.

The Effects of Incarceration on the Community

Because of the massive increase in the prison population in recent years, there are more people leaving prison than ever before (Petersilia 2008). The communities the hardest hit by the trend toward mass incarceration are those that are predominantly African-American. The War on Drugs, mandatory minimum sentences, and other sentence enhancements are primarily to blame, but increased law enforcement efforts have also contributed (Wacquant 2001, Goode 2002, Mauer 2011). In some communities, as many as 15 percent of the young African-American male population is incarcerated at any given time, and when compared with their white counterparts, African-American males are six times more likely to serve at least one year in prison (Petersilia 2008).

The African-American children residing in these communities are therefore significantly more likely to have one parent, two parents or multiple family members behind bars (Wakefield and Wildeman 2011). Communities with the highest rates of incarceration also have the lowest rates of marriage (Travis 2008), and many children growing up in these neighborhoods reside in households headed by a single mother (Thomas, Farrell and Barnes 1996). By concentrating large numbers of individuals from particular neighborhoods and communities, the informal social control mechanisms are greatly reduced (Mauer 2006b).

The end result is that some communities of lower socioeconomic status are fraught with households that are disrupted by incarceration. Upon their release from prison, inmates will carry many of the same behaviors back to the community that resulted in their initial incarceration. This issue is further exacerbated by a determinate sentencing structure, which means that people return to their community, regardless of whether they are physically and emotionally ready to be reintegrated (Petersilia 2008). Many inmates do not receive rehabilitation programming while incarcerated, and thus rely on the same mechanisms to solve problems as they previously relied on, such as violence, dealing drugs and involvement with gangs (Stowell and Byrne 2008).

Another collateral consequence of imprisonment for these communities that is often overlooked is how they are affected by funding. Prison construction is typically completed in rural communities, and once prisoners, most of who are from urban areas, are housed in these facilities, the census officially counts them as residing in the community in which the prison is located. Both federal and state funds are based on population numbers. As such, the money that could potentially be invested into communities that are the most in need lose the money that could be used to help revive the social and economic conditions. The rural areas, which are already benefitting from having the prison enhance the workforce in the area, are retaining more money for their communities (Kappeler and Potter 2005).

The Effects of Violence on the Community

what type of person do I want standing next to me in the grocery store? Do I want that person to have access to rehabilitation programs in prison? Perhaps he learned to read and write or gained some valuable work skills. Or do I want that person to have suffered long-term physical or sexual abuse in prison? Do I want her to have kicked her drug or alcohol addiction or to have joined a prison gang? (Trammell 2012: 15)

As the above quote perfectly illustrates, an individual carries his or her experiences from prison to their communities when they return. Positive experiences, such as participation in rehabilitation, treatment, vocational or educational programs are more likely to desist from crime and successfully reintegrate back into their communities. Conversely, exposure to negative experiences, such as antisocial behavior and violence are likely to prevent successful reintegration and lead to continuation, and potentially more severe, of criminal activity.

From a community standpoint, it must be remembered that communities are comprised of networks of individuals and family units. There is a reasonable amount research on the effects that the disruption of prison has on the community. But, what about the effects of prison violence on the community? It can be assumed that communities are negatively influenced by an individual's violence experiences. When considering that large numbers of individuals from particular communities are incarcerated and likely exposed to violence, the results direr.

These communities are quickly becoming breeding grounds for even more crime and violence. Intergenerational crime and violence, especially when coupled with peer influences, is likely spreading throughout these communities. When crime, deviance and violence becomes the norm, these communities are left with little hope of recovery, and the citizens residing in these communities are destined to repeat similar patterns in future generations.

The Effects of Incarceration on Society

Many may cling to previously held beliefs that criminals are qualitatively different than "the rest of society". As often rings true with retributive punishment ideals, many of these same people believe that those who commit criminal offenses make the rational decision to do so. Similarly, the families of these offenders make a conscious decision to maintain contact with them, even after they are released from prison. Community members make the decision to allow these offenders back into their neighborhoods, or they choose to not move from these areas, which are riddled with crime and violence. As members of the larger society, many believe that by continuing along the same path of mass incarceration, we are free of the larger effects of prisons and jails.

This, however, couldn't be further from the truth. Financially, we support our incarceration binge and all the monetary costs that coincide with it. Changes in the types of individuals we are incarcerating create an additional financial burden, as we struggle to care for inmates who are mentally ill, of poor physical health or aging. Even without these medical costs, the cost of maintaining a correctional facility is significant, and more prisoners equate to more expense.

The mass incarceration movement has changed society in other ways. There is perhaps no greater example than examining the changes made to the voting population in the United States. Consider the number of young, African-American males who have lost their ability to vote for the remainder of their lifetime, often as a result of committing a nonviolent felony. This will have a lasting effect on the political landscape of the country.

The Effects of Violence on Society

There have been no studies to date that examine how exposure to prison violence affects society at large. Knowledge of the prison experience prompts the speculation that ultimately, "society is faced with a population of (primarily) men who have been physically, psychologically and socially harmed" (Pratt 2009: 83). This burden does not stop at the community level. There are greater implications for a society that must contend with these effects.

Perhaps one of the most devastating effects is the potential for additional unchecked exposure to violence and desensitization has been well documented. Although once released from prison most inmates return to their respective communities, these communities do not function in a vacuum. Norms and values are transmitted from communities to prison, from prison to communities, and from communities and prisons to the larger society. This may occur as residents either move beyond their communities or communicate with those outside of their communities. It may also be a result of the transmission of prison-based images to popular media and culture. One only need examine the prison references in movies, television shows, video games and music to see that the transmission of this culture began to occur many years ago. There is little doubt that anyone serving a prison sentence expects to find violence engrained into the prison culture upon their arrival, even if they have never been directly exposed to a correctional facility.

Conclusion

Incarceration certainly negatively affects individuals, families, communities and society as a whole. Apart from the large number of prisoners, their experiences while they are incarcerated can ultimately have a greater effect. Negative experiences, such as those rooted in violence, are likely to result in highly damaged individuals being returned to society. In contrast, positive experiences, such as those that focus on rehabilitation, education and treatment, will be more likely to result in inmates successfully reintegrating into their community and becoming contributing members of society.

Chapter 6
Challenges to Understanding the Problem

Introduction

If prison violence creates so many problems, why has it not been studied more thoroughly? Like many issues, an increase in understanding often leads to an increase in both prevention and treatment of problems. However, understanding the violence that occurs behind the walls of prisons is fraught with obstacles and difficulties. As will be discussed throughout this chapter, inmates are unlikely to report being victimized, making it impossible for correctional authorities to gauge the true extent of the problem or to sanction those who perpetrate violence. Correctional officers may feel apathetic about the issue, and with the correctional officer to inmate ratio being low, it is understandably difficult to monitor and prevent potential violent acts. The public also is unlikely to offer concern for this issue, and therefore little has been done policy wise for prevention or treatment for those who have been victimized behind bars.

Reporting Issues

When comparing crime rates between the Uniform Crime Report (UCR) and the National Crime Victimization Survey (NCVS), it is apparent that crime in the general community is vastly underreported. Those that are the least likely to be officially reported are crimes that occur between acquaintances. This is especially true for personal crimes, such as robbery and sexual assault, two crimes that are particularly rampant among the inmate population.

Just as in the free community, acts that are more violent are more likely to be reported. Data on inmate deaths while incarcerated are compiled by the institution and are readily available. Examining state prisoner deaths reveals that in 2009, the leading cause of inmate deaths were illness related, comprising more than 88 percent of the total number of deaths. Cancer, heart disease and other illnesses, including influenza, cerebrovascular disease and cirrhosis, are almost equally distributed within this category. Suicides account for just under 6 percent, and homicides for 1.6 percent of deaths (Noonan and Carson 2011). (See Table 6.1). Although some may interpret these findings as indicators of low levels of violence, in actuality they reveal only that such violence is unlikely to be fatal. Considering the number of correctional staff present to help diffuse physical altercations before they escalate, and the fear of potential lawsuits that may result from deaths in custody, these findings are not surprising.

Table 6.1   State prisoner deaths (2009)

Causes	Number	Percentage of Total Deaths
All	3,408	100
Illness	3,014	88.4
Heart disease	870	25.5
Cancer	911	26.7
Liver disease	258	7.6
AIDS related	94	2.8
Other illness	881	25.9
Suicide	201	5.9
Homicide	55	1.6
Drug/Alcohol intoxication	50	1.5
Accident	31	0.9
Other/unknown	57	1.7

Source: Noonan and Carson 2011

www.bjs.gov/content/pub/pdf/pjdc0009st.pdf

Although reasonably reliable data exists for homicides within correctional facilities, no reliable data exists on nonlethal forms of violence (Gibbons 2011). Reporting rates vary by the type of victimization experienced. In their examination of relatively minor victimizations, O'Donnell and Edgar (1998) found that about 25 percent of inmates report being a victim of a theft, 14 percent of assault, 13 percent of a verbal threat and 12 percent of verbal abuse. When comparing official reports with victim surveys, rates of physical assault vary. Between 0.25 percent and 0.45 percent of inmates officially report being physically assaulted, while victim surveys indicate these numbers are much greater, ranging from 10 percent to 32 percent (Bowker 1980b, Cooley 1993, McCorkle, Miethe and Drass 1995, O'Donnell and Edgar 1996, Woolredge 1998, Perez, Gover, Tennyson and Santos 2010). One only needs to examine the data that indicate that there were absolutely no physical assaults reported in state prisons in Arkansas, North Dakota or South Dakota during the year 2000 (Gibbons 2011) to realize the flawed nature of official reports. Similarly, recent research claims that somewhere in the very wide range of between 4 percent and 40 percent of inmates have been sexual assault victims (Gaes and

Goldberg 2004, Beck and Harrison 2007, Beck, Harrison, Berzofsky, Caspar and Krebs 2010). However, many victims of sexual assault state that they have never discussed their victimization experiences with anyone (Struckman-Johnson et al. 1996), let alone officially report the offense to correctional authorities.

Community level reporting issues are magnified among members of the prison community. Being in constant close proximity to the assailant in a culture that promotes self-reliance, retaliation and masculinity creates an environment where reporting victimization is discouraged. Many of the reasons inmates don't report victimization herald back to the tenets of the convict code, such as embarrassment, fear of harassment, or fear of retaliation from either the assailant or other inmates. Other reasons may include not wanting assignment to protective custody housing units, or believing that correctional staff will not assist them or take their seriously.

Being violently victimized can be a humiliating and emasculating experience. In light of the emphasis placed on the prison hierarchy and exerting one's own toughness, it seems intuitive that an inmate would be hesitant to report his or her victimization experiences. Not only could the inmate feel ridiculed by their fellow inmates, but it would also mean admitting victimization to correctional staff, who are also likely male.

Although embarrassment potentially exists as a barrier to reporting any form of victimization, it is an especially prominent factor in the lack of reporting for incidents involving sexual victimization (Levan-Miller 2010). Sexual victimization can be particularly emasculating (Knowles 1999, Man and Cronan 2001, Donaldson 2003, Hensley et al. 2003), and victims fear other inmates perceiving them as either homosexual or weaker than their fellow inmates. The convict code specifies that inmates should show no signs of weakness, and, in an environment where respect is seen as currency, inmates fear that sexual victimization in particular may lead to a loss of respect and extreme embarrassment (Knowles 1999, Man and Cronan 2001).

Not only do inmates fear embarrassment, but they also fear that revealing their victimization experiences may lead to harassment by other inmates, as well as retaliation and repeated victimization at the hands of the original perpetrator (Levan-Miller 2010). Once they have been labeled as a target by the correctional population, they will likely continue to be harassed and victimized (Mariner 2001, Hassine 2010).

Others who have been severely victimized, either with a singular incident, or as a result of repeated violent victimizations, may be eligible to be placed in safekeeping. While this may seem like a preventative solution for future potential abuse, victims may feel as though safekeeping is more of a punishment. In addition to those in safekeeping having fewer privileges (Dumond 2000, Struckman-Johnson and Struckman-Johnson 2000, Hensley et al. 2003), many fear abusive or inadequate treatment while housed in protective custody (Alarid 2000, O'Donnell 2004). When considering this as a reason for nonreporting of sexual violence in particular, this reason has been closely associated with those who self-identify as either homosexual or bisexual, as well as other characteristics (Levan-Miller 2010). See Chapter 7 for a full discussion on protective custody.

Reporting issues may also be problematic when behaviors are ambiguously violent. Several types of activities may be perceived as those in which there is no clearly defined victim and offender, or those that border being nonviolent activities. In addition to some forms of sexual abuse, such as those involving coercion rather than force, behaviors that are often classified as "bullying" also sometimes fit this category. The notion of bullying has been criticized as being "inherently contentious, ambiguous and of limited utility" (Edgar et al. 2003: 23). Bullying encompasses a broad range of behaviors, including spreading rumors, playing practical jokes, intimidation, name-calling, harassment and physical assault (Olweus 1994, Ireland and Archer 1996, Ireland 1997, as cited in Ireland and Ireland 2006).

Reporting behaviors may also be influenced by demographic factors, such as race and ethnicity. However, this is also tempered by whether the alleged assailant is another inmate or correctional staff. White inmates have been shown to be more inclined to report a physical or sexual victimization perpetrated by other inmates, while African-American inmates are more likely to report being victimized by correctional staff. Hispanic inmates, in contrast, show above average reporting rates for victimization from both fellow inmates and staff than both White and African-American inmates (Wolff, Shi and Blitz 2008).

This information elucidates further questions as to whether these inmates are more likely to be victimized by these particular groups, or are simply more likely to report offenses committed by the respective perpetrators. For instance, do Hispanics suffer from more victimization by inmates and staff, or are they less likely to feel prisonized and connected to the prison environment than White and African-American inmates? Ultimately, official reporting behaviors often present a complicated picture as to whether they represent true victimization, or simply a greater propensity for particular demographics to be more likely to report victimization experiences against certain groups of offenders.

Issues with Correctional Staff

The relationship between correctional staff and inmates also should be considered. Many inmates perceive correctional officers as the enemy, and do not trust them in personal matters, such as violent victimization. Officially reporting violence could put corrupt correctional staff in a position to take advantage of them. As Ross indicates "some COs have been known to initiate violence, for example, by putting two cons who hate each other together in the same cell and sitting back to watch the fireworks" (2008: 83).

Issues with correctional officers are exacerbated when considering sexually assaultive behavior. Staff has raised concerns that many claims of victimization are either unfounded or unsubstantiated (Beck, Harrison and Adams 2009). Exposure to what have been deemed falsified reports may lead to their not acknowledging sexual assault as problematic (Banbury 2004). Many also cite difficulty in knowing whether sexual activities are consensual or forced (Owen and Wells 2006, Owen, McCampbell and Wells 2007). Furthermore, although sexual misconduct has historically been an issue, it has only recently been brought to the public forefront. As such, many correctional officers report a lack of experience in dealing with sexual violence (Owen and Wells 2006).

In terms of reporting sexual victimization, inmates seem more willing to report incidents perpetrated by correctional staff than other inmates. A 2007 Bureau of Justice Statistics report indicates that of the 60,500 incidents, 27,500 were perpetrated by fellow inmates, while 38,600 were perpetrated by staff (Beck and Harrison 2007). In should be noted, however, that inmate-on-inmate incidents only include nonconsensual sexual acts and abusive sexual contacts. In contrast, staff misconduct includes a much wider range of behaviors, some of which may include those that are routine to the operation of a prison, such as cavity and strip searches. (See Table 6.2).

Table 6.2   State and federal prisoners reporting sexual victimization (2007)

Type	Number	Percent
Total	60,500	4.50
Inmate on inmate	27,500	2.10
Nonconsensual sexual acts	16,800	1.30
Abusive sexual contacts only	10,600	0.80
Staff sexual misconduct	38,600	2.90
Unwilling activity	22,600	1.70
Excluding touching	16,900	1.30
Touching only	5,700	0.40
Willing activity	22,700	1.70
Excluding touching	20,600	1.50
Touching only	2,100	0.20

Source: Beck and Harrison 2007

bjs.ojp.usdoj.gov/content/pub/pdf/svsfpri07.pdf

Public Perceptions

Research has found that the public is relatively unfamiliar with criminal justice issues and policies (Chapman, Mirrlees-Black and Brown 2002). The public is generally unconcerned over issues related to incarcerated populations. Because of the movement toward punitiveness and incapacitation and away from rehabilitation, most people are more than willing to lock away those who have committed wrongdoing. Ultimately, because the public's focus tends to be retributive, policy makers seem to have been given a free pass on issues concerning inmate welfare. This trend is certainly nothing new. Historically, a "lack of public scrutiny and political accountability, alongside collective ambivalence and indifference, explains in part how psychiatric and penal institutions sustained excessively punitive and often unlawful practices" (McCulloch and Scraton 2009: 2).

From the public's viewpoint, the more controlling the confinement, the more effective it will be at curbing inappropriate inmate behavior (Pizarro, Stenius and Pratt 2006). Those considered the most dangerous offenders are given solitary confinement, or placed in supermaximum security prisons. These are the inmates the public is the least concerned with rehabilitating, as they are viewed as beyond hope or simply not worthy of rehabilitation (Rhodes 2004, as cited in Scraton 2009, Pizarro et al. 2006). By labeling those who are already considered criminals as being the worst of the worst, it is easier for their abuse to be justified (Terry 2000, 2003). Not only are the most severe housing situations ineffective at rehabilitation efforts, but they also do little to reduce institutional violence and, in some cases, may increase levels of violence (Briggs, Sundt and Castellano 2003, Pizarro et al 2006).

Why has the public become so misinformed on issues related to incarceration? The answer may lie, in part, on the lack of focus given to these issues by the news media. As a result, the public relies on accounts that are provided by popular media outlets, such as television shows and movies. These venues provide highly sensationalized and fictionalized accounts of what occurs in prisons (Levenson 2001, Mason 2003, Bennett 2006, Meiners 2007). Prison violence, especially prison rape, has become so pervasive that it exists not only in dramatic depictions, as in movies such as the *Shawshank Redemption* (1994) and *Sleepers* (1996), and the television show *Oz* (1997–2003), but also in comedic portrayals, including *Let's Go To Prison* (2006), *There's Something About Mary* (1998) and *Office Space* (1999) (Levan, Polzer and Downing 2011).

The very few non-fictionalized accounts of prisons are those that depict extreme violence among inmates, often at the expense of correctional staff or visitors. For instance, riots, such as the one that occurred at Attica, receive significant news coverage (Reiman and Leighton 2010). The very few successful escapes, such as the infamous "Texas Seven" escape that occurred in 2000, may receive both news coverage and, in this instance, be featured on programs such as *America's Most Wanted* (Notorious Texas Seven 2008). These types of high profile and rare occurrences are often the only primary "real life" exposure that the general public has to inmates.

Byrne and Hummer (2007) illustrate the pervasive nature of the existence of prison violence. Comedians, such as Chris Rock, humorously "raise important, but often troubling, questions about what the public expects – and indeed hopes – will happen to offenders in our federal and state prison system today" (532). In short, both the fictionalized and non-fictionalized accounts portray all inmates as being inherently evil and violent and deserving of the most punitive measures available.

This, combined with the news media coverage falsely depicting crime as ever increasing, has also contributed to the public's tough attitudes toward crime and punishment. Ultimately, the media may be partially responsible for the growth in the United States prison population (Mathieson 2001, Mauer 2001), a trend that is beginning to be duplicated in other nations as well, as discussed in Chapter 3 (Cavadino and Dignan 2006).

Inmates themselves also gain insight into the prison world through media depictions, as well as accounts from their acquaintances who have served time. Kreinert and Fleisher (2005) argue that prison violence, especially sexual violence, has begun to take on the characteristics of an urban legend.

Inmates say they learn about prison rape from television shows and from cronies, family and friends who've been to prison (or not), and in long periods in jails, where "old school" inmates relish terrorizing young inmates with tales of prison rape, boys and daddies, sex slavery and queens running rampant in short skirts carrying purses. Then, when they arrive at new-inmate orientation they are likely to be told that they'll be raped or someone will sexually manipulate them and they'll end up repaying cigarette, candy and gambling debts with sexual acts (3).

Despite the attempts made by policy makers and the public to separate completely prisons and their captive populations from mainstream society, this does not seem to be entirely the case. Unfortunately, once policies have shifted to focus on retribution and punishment, it is very difficult to shift to a softer approach. Politicians know that the public will be generally unsupportive of approaches that are seen as "softer" on criminals, such as those that focus on rehabilitation or intermediate sanctions. Prison populations are influenced by both a lack of concern for their welfare, and the punitive attitudes by the public. The result of this lack of concern returns to the community in the form of inmates that are perhaps irreversibly damaged.

Conclusion

In addition to other issues, prison is a world far removed from the free society, both physically and emotionally. Once someone becomes an inmate, the general society ceases to be concerned with his or her well-being. They are then placed in a world where their welfare is entirely in the hands of correctional staff. The nexus of the issues related to the prison system contributes to a lack of concern or understanding of the unique issues faced by modern inmates. Although the authors of this statement wrote their article three decades ago, and were primarily focused with sexual assault, their concerns still ring true today: "discovery and documentation of this behavior are compromised by the nature of prison conditions, inmate codes and subculture and staff attitudes" (Cotton and Groth 1982: 48).

Chapter 7
What is Being Done?

Introduction

Administrators have long recognized the existence of violence in correctional facilities. Many of the existing formal control mechanisms are in place in order to prevent inmates from engaging in violence against one another and correctional staff. Correctional officer training is also tailored to address some of these issues. Inmates themselves may also take steps to informally deal with and prevent being violently victimized.

Classification

Depending on the type of offense committed, an inmate will either be housed in a federal or state-level institution. In order to be housed in a federal facility, an individual must have committed a federal crime. Although crimes such as kidnapping and bank robbery have traditionally been associated with federal prisons, the federalization of drug crimes means that now federal prisons are housing a substantial number of drug offenders (Sabol and West 2009). Depending on the determined level of risk of escape or violence, federal prisoners may be housed at one of several levels, ranging from minimum security to administrative segregation. Although administrative, or supermaximum security facilities, contain the fewest number of inmates housed in the federal system, more than 25,000 inmates are currently housed at this security level (Tewksbury 2010).

In contrast, those housed at the state level are predominantly violent offenders, comprising approximately 60 percent of the total state prison population (Sabol and West 2009). Inmates are assigned to minimum-, medium- or maximum-security level prisons. Regardless of whether they are a federal or a state inmate, their classification continues upon their arrival at the individual prison in a process known as institutional level classification.

Institutional level classification considers several factors. First, the internal security, or the likelihood the individual will engage in violence or misconduct (Sorenson and Cunningham 2010), often considers both an inmate's characteristics, such as their age, as well as factors related to their current offense, such as the sentence length (Berk, Kriegler and Baek 2006). Also, officials consider factors related to external security, such as the likelihood of escape, and individual inmate needs, including programming needs, such as education or treatment (Sorenson and Cunningham 2010). By taking all these factors into consideration, correctional authorities hope to be able to predict which inmates are the most likely perpetrators of violence in an effort to reduce the likelihood of inmate-generated violent activities. However, many find fault with the existing classification system.

The current system has been criticized as not being able to adequately predict which inmates will engage in violence (Berk et al. 2006). The inmates who are the most likely to receive the harshest sentence, murderers, would also be the most likely to be classified at a higher security institution, or within a unit that is of higher security within an institution. Inmates currently serving time for murder, however, are less likely to engage in institutional violence when compared with other types of offenders (Sorenson and Cunningham 2010). When specifically examining sexual violence, it has been found that those who are the most likely assailants are not only those who have been sexually victimized themselves, but also have a history of predatory behavior while incarcerated. In fact, sentence length seems to be a key variable; for each additional year incarcerated, the likelihood of perpetrating a sexual offense increases by 15.5 percent (Morash, Jeong and Zang 2010). More restrictive housing does not decrease institutional misconduct, and placing inmates in lower levels of security than the classification procedures recommend may not lead to increased levels of institutional misconduct (Bench and Allen 2003, Camp and Gaes 2005, as cited in Byrne and Hummer 2008)

Moreover, the same risk-classification instrument is used for both male and female inmates, despite the fact that there are stark differences between the two sexes (Harer and Langan 2001). Not only are they incarcerated for different types of offenses, but there are also differences in how males and females experience prison and the types of programming requirements needed for rehabilitation and reintegration. For instance, because female are less likely to commit violence while incarcerated, there may be concern that we are "over classifying" female inmates (Harer and Langan 2001). Females may be being housed at security levels that do not consider their differences from male inmates, perhaps stunting their rehabilitation experiences. Females who are housed in higher level security institutions than needed may be less likely to receive the treatment or socialization necessary to aid in their successful return to society. Additionally, female inmates who are overly aggressive and violent cannot be segregated from the general population due to space limitations (Pogrebin and Dodge 2001).

It may be that these classification routines are little more than ceremony. Facilities or wings may be classified appropriate for an inmate's security level based on factors such as availability of space, or the neighborhood from which the offender heralds (Hassine 2010). While these considerations are important for practical purposes, they should not be the primary deciding factor for classification purposes, especially given the importance classification has on an inmate's road to rehabilitation. Researchers fault current classification systems as being based on poor-quality research and thus being ineffective at predicting which inmates are the most at risk to commit violence while incarcerated (Byrne and Hummer 2008).

Supermax Facilities

Forty-four states in the United States currently have a supermaximum security, or administrative segregation, facility (Tewksbury 2010). These facilities are reserved for those who are deemed the most dangerous and the most likely to engage in violence while incarcerated, including those serving long sentences for violent offenses, known gang members, and those who have had multiple violent disciplinary issues while incarcerated (Lovell, Cloyes, Allen and Rhodes 2000, Wang, Owens, Long, Diamond and Smith 2000, Tewksbury 2010).

The rationale behind assigning an inmate to a supermax facility is obvious. By placing the most violent, dangerous inmates in highly restrictive living conditions, it is believed that they will have fewer opportunities to commit violence against other inmates, as well as correctional staff. Movement in these institutions is highly restricted; inmates are often confined to their cells for 23 hours a day and are placed in an external cage-like cell during their "yard time".

Although supermax facilities do boast lower inmate-on-staff assaults, there seems to be little to no effect on the prevalence of inmate-on-inmate assaults (Sundt, Castellano and Briggs 2008). As Hartman (2008) indicates "The only behavior it seems to actually deter is that which could result in the successful transition from prison to free society" (172). Inmates placed in these units are often provided little to no rehabilitation opportunities. This, combined with a lack of socialization, means they are even more ill equipped to return to society.

The boom in the building of supermax facilities was a direct result of the punitive political climate. The end result was the construction of more supermax facilities than was needed to house the justifiably more dangerous populations. As a result, those housed in lower security prisons who are seen as problematic, including the mentally ill, may be transferred to these facilities (Kappeler and Potter 2005). Supermax facilities are therefore housing populations that are not inherently violent, as they were originally intended. (See Figure 7.1, page 86)

Much of the reasoning behind the supermax ideal seems to herald back to the "separate and silent" prisons, as developed in the Pennsylvania system in the 1800s. The emphasis on keeping inmates completely isolated began to take a toll on inmates, contributing to many becoming mentally ill. As Hartman's quote illustrates, supermax facilities may be mimicking the Pennsylvania system and doing more harm than good. Extended periods of isolation often lead to what Perkinson (1994) refers to as "SHU syndrome", or security housing unit syndrome, which he found present in the majority of inmates housed Pelican Bay facility in California. Supermax facilities have been shown to increase an inmate's disorientation, anger, rage, anxiety and a host of other psychiatric issues (Tewksbury 2010), increasing their potential for violence upon their release (Austin and Irwin 2012).

At age seventeen, Brian Nelson was sentenced to twenty-six years in prison after being found guilty of armed robbery and murder. He was originally sent to Stateville Correctional Center in Illinois, where he escaped. Once he was back in custody, he was transferred to a few different facilities before he landed in a minimum security prison in New Mexico. Although he is known to have had no disciplinary issues in New Mexio, he was unexpectedly transferred to Tamms Correctional Center in Illinois, a supermaximum security facility, where he resided until he was released just a few years ago.

Tamms is one of fourteen state facilities that Illinois Governor Pat Quinn recently announced as being planned to be shut down. Tamms houses many high profile criminals, including Henry Brison (the "I-57 Killer"), serial child rapist John Spires, and Michael "Paradise" Johnson (Gangster Disciple leader). Like other supermaximum security facilities, Tamms is meant to house problematic and violent inmates that are viewed as being beyond the scope of supervision in other correctional facilities.

As Tamms and other supermax facilities come under fire by organizations such as Amnesty International and the American Civil Liberties Union for potential Eight Amendment violations, it remains a mystery as to why some inmates, such as Nelson, have been transferred to the institution. Although he was convicted of two violent crimes, supermaximum security seems overzealous. He attributes his post-incarceration mental illnesses, including Post-Traumatic Stress Disorder, depression and anxiety, to the isolation and harsh treatment of the facility.

Figure 7.1   The controversy of supermax facilities

Sources: McKinney 2012, I'm still in that box 2012

Protective Custody

While those inmates who prison administrators deem as the most likely to be dangerous or violet are placed in administrative segregation or secure housing units, those who are more likely targets of victimization are more likely to be placed in protective custody. Inmates who fear violent victimization can request to be placed in protective custody. Some examples of inmates who may be routinely placed in protective custody include those who cooperate with correctional officers by snitching on fellow inmates, those who are routinely victimized by other inmates, or those who have committed types of crimes that make them more vulnerable targets, such as crimes against children. At any given time, there are approximately 5,000 inmates housed in protective custody units nationwide (Camp and Camp 2001).

The rationale behind protective custody is logical: by isolating those who are the most at risk of violent victimization, not only should rates of violence decrease, but inmates who are the most likely to be victimized should have their fears and anxiety alleviated. The reality of protective custody, however, is that it can actually be quite punitive. At-risk inmates specifically do not request separate housing because of a lack of education and treatment programs available, fewer work opportunities and fewer opportunities to attend religious services (Lockwood 1980, Wooden and Parker 1982, Dumond 2000, Struckman-Johnson and Struckman-Johnson 2000, Man and Cronan 2001, Hensley, Tewksbury and Castle 2003). Ultimately, these inmates are being further punished when they have committed no additional infractions. By limiting contact with others and offering reduced programming, these inmates are treated just as severely as those who have committed disciplinary infractions or who are housed in administrative segregation (Browne, Cambier and Agha 2011).

There is another aspect of protective custody that is even more controversial and disturbing. Some correctional officers who supervise those in protective custody may be doling out their own version of extralegal punishments. For instance, some inmates fear that these correctional officers may intentionally leave cell doors unlocked for predators or that they may temporarily sell vulnerable inmates to others (Money and Bohmer 1980, Alarid 2000, O'Donnell 2004). This may be more likely to occur for inmates who both other inmates and correctional staff are equally likely to detest, such as those who have committed offenses against children.

The fears of inmates seem to be echoed in my study on reasons for inmates to not report sexual victimization (Levan-Miller 2010). Although a small percentage of the sample cited this as the primary reason, those who did elect this option seem to display similar characteristics. This option is correlated with inmates who self-identify as homosexual or bisexual, are African-American or Hispanic or who reside in correctional facilities with larger numbers of correctional officers.

If protective custody is to be used, several changes should be made to make it a more viable option for those who are targeted for violent victimization. Blatant disregard for inmate safety, especially when correctional officers are involved, must be addressed. Perhaps special training and education for those selected for protective custody units should be mandated. Another important revision would be to make work and treatment opportunities more readily available to these inmates. Having separate treatment, religious services and education areas, as well as specially supervised work shifts, would allow these inmates to more fully participate in activities that will ultimately help them to be rehabilitated.

Solutions to Gangs

Gangs continue to be a pervasive issue for correctional facilities. Although it is impossible to know the exact number of inmates who are affiliated with a gang there is no denying their presence and their involvement in violent activities. Since the emergence of the first known prison gangs decades ago in California, many solutions have been implemented to try to reduce the number of gang members and their influence on the prison culture.

Initially, correctional facilities use databases to track and monitor prison groups and their activities. Not only can they track the identity of the gang members, but also the types of criminal activities they have been involved in, as well as any identifying marks, such as tattoos. A major advantage to database tracking in the technological age is that information can be shared among agencies (Levan 2011). Correctional facilities can share information on inmates with each other to determine potential gang activities, as well as be equipped with information on incoming inmates in cases of a facility transfer. Furthermore, this information can be communicated to police agencies upon the release of these inmates from prison.

Segregating known gang members is another approach. The potential effect of segregation may be seen in the drastic decline in the number of prison homicides in the past several decades (Gibbons 2011). When comparing homicide rates from 1980 to those in 2002, there has been a 93 percent decrease among state inmates (Mumola 2005). This may be partially attributed to segregation of gang members, as it makes orchestrating group violence more difficult. Additionally, placing known gang members in administrative segregation reduces their opportunities to commit acts of violence against members of rival gangs.

There is a fine line between segregating gang members and racial segregation. Although gang segregation is a generally accepted practice, racial desegregation has been occurring among prison populations for the past few decades (Trulson, Marquart, Hemmens and Carroll 2008). A recent court ruling (*Johnson v. California* 2005) illustrates this point. Johnson argued that segregating inmates based on race is a violation of his equal protection rights guaranteed under the Fourteenth Amendment. The court stated that there must be a compelling interest to racially segregate inmates, and should only be implemented if it is the only way to accomplish the goals of the correctional facility, such as rehabilitation, security and control (Trulson et al. 2008).

The court ruling places issues involving segregation in a precarious state. Racial composition is often the determining factor in gang affiliation. But, institutions are prevented from segregating based on race unless absolutely necessary. Trulson and his colleagues (2008) explain this conundrum best when they indicate, "Race functions as a proxy for gang membership, and gang membership is used as a proxy for violence" (273).

Another recent solution has been the creation of gang-free facilities. In order to be eligible for housing in a gang-free facility, inmates must not have a history of gang affiliation, or any involvement in gang activities. These facilities can provide nonviolent and safe environment for inmates, potentially preventing them from feeling the need to join a gang for protection (Levan 2011). Because this is a relatively new effort, it remains to be seen whether this is an effective means to prevent gang violence.

Despite the obvious reasons for reducing gang activity in prisons, some have touted the benefits of the existence of gangs in prisons. They may serve as a means of informal social control among the inmates. They provide a set of norms and values for the inmates, and provide a group setting for those who have been outcast from mainstream society (Levan 2011). Inmates may view gangs as functional and fear that their removal may increase the formal social control exerted by correctional staff (Rivera, Cowles and Dorman 2003).

Correctional officers may also see a benefit to allowing prison gangs to exist. Not only do they potentially decrease the formal social control needed to control inmates, but they also may deflect violence away from correctional staff (Gilligan 2002). The existence of prison gangs allows the confrontational mentality to endure among inmates. The mentality may prevent inmates from engaging in violence against correctional officers.

Initiatives for HIV/AIDS-infected Inmates

In recent years, prisons have enacted new policies to deal with the emergence of those who have contracted HIV and AIDS. Facilities prevent inmates from engaging in risky behaviors, such as tattooing, sexual activities and drug use. In recognizing that many inmates may not obey these institutional rules, some facilities have taken more proactive steps to attempt to reduce the spread of infection among inmates.

Mandatory testing is one initiative that has been implemented. In 2008, 23 states tested all inmates during the admission process. Five states tested all inmates at some point while they were serving their sentence, and six states conducted testing during the release process. Inmates who either request testing or who show symptoms of infections are given tests in the federal prison system, as well as in all state prison systems (Maruschak 2009). The obvious advantages to mandatory testing are identification of infected inmates in order to provide appropriate medical treatment. A potential disadvantage is that testing may lull the correctional administrators and staff, as well as the inmates, into a false sense of security, potentially encouraging risky behaviors (Blumberg and Laster 2009). Symptoms of HIV and AIDS may take time to surface, leading many to believe that inmates who are indeed infected are disease free.

Closely related to the idea of mandatory testing is segregation for infected inmates. Once testing has revealed that an inmate is infected with HIV or AIDS, they may be placed into separate wings of the facility to discourage the spread of the disease. However, many have raised concerns over the potential for poor treatment and substandard living conditions for those who have been identified and segregated (Blumberg and Laster 2009).

Another tactic adopted by a few states is to make condoms available to all inmates. Among a few conscientious inmates who are engaging in consensual sex, this may help prevent the spread of HIV and AIDS. However, this solution seems to ignore the violent and impulsive nature of sexual assault. Few assailants will stop to obtain and put on a condom before the transaction. Condoms may also be used as weapons. They may be used to strangle other inmates or correctional staff, or "could be filled with sand or dirt and used to hit other inmates or correctional staff" (Nerenberg 2002). There is also concern that providing condoms to inmates will imply that sexual activity is condoned by the institutions (Nerenberg 2002, Blumberg and Laster 2009).

Sex Offender Treatment

As the population of sex offenders in prison has increased, so has the need for sex offender treatment. Many barriers exist for effective treatment. One is the need for offenders to disclose all of their offenses committed, regardless of whether the criminal justice system is aware of each offense. This disclosure may result in either denial of parole or more strict parole restrictions upon release (Kersting 2003). Those completing therapy are therefore hesitant to disclose such information, which likely impedes their recovery.

Because sex offenders are more likely to be victimized or to fear victimization while incarcerated, they are more likely to be placed in protective custody. Once removed from the general prison population, any type of treatment program becomes more difficult to implement. This is especially problematic considering many of the therapies offered in the prison setting are delivered in a group environment, and many protective custody units are not designed to hold group sessions.

Finally, as with all treatment efforts, there is an expense involved. What makes treatment for sexual offenders particularly problematic is that it is not as accepted by the public as treatment for other types of offenders. Because the public believes the widespread and erroneous notion that sex offenders have higher recidivism rates, they are unlikely to support taxpayer money being allocated toward their rehabilitation efforts (Holmes and Holmes 2009).

Closed-circuit Television Systems

Many modern prisons take advantage of technological advances by implementing closed-circuit television (CCTV) systems. Based on deterrence and situational crime prevention approaches, CCTV is meant to increase the amount and level of surveillance that correctional officers and staff have over inmates. Furthermore, by altering an inmate's physical environment, the opportunities to commit crime can be reduced (Cornish and Clark 2003, Allard, Wortley and Stewart 2008, Lippert 2009).

CCTV systems have some major limitations. Because correctional staff do not watch the monitors constantly, they may be ineffective at preventing offenses. As such, surveillance systems are considered more of a reactive approach rather than a proactive one (Turner 2007). Capturing images of criminal activity is a valuable tool in terms of investigation and prosecution (Turner 2007), but as a preventative measure, many existing CCTV measures cannot accomplish this task.

One answer to the lack of surveillance is the installation of Automated Video Surveillance (AVS) systems. This approach is different from traditional CCTV initiatives in that it does not require constant surveillance. These systems can automatically detect security threats that occur within the periphery of the camera. The system then sounds an alarm to alert correctional staff so that they can respond appropriately and in a timely fashion (Turner 2007).

Little research has been undertaken to determine whether CCTV is an effective tool to prevent inmate misconduct. Recent research shows surveillance systems are more effective at preventing nonviolent than violent behaviors. Inmate threats against staff are not significantly influenced by the presence of CCTV. Planned inmate on inmate assaults are more likely to be thwarted by cameras than those that occur spontaneously (Allard, Wortley and Stewart 2008). Inmates wanting to avoid detection and sanctioning are likely to move planned assaults or fights to individual cells (Trammell 2012). Short of installation of cameras in every cell and location in a facility, CCTV cannot prevent the majority of violence among inmates.

Decades ago, Foucault described the idea of the Panopticon. The Panopticon-style prison is one that allows for constant surveillance. According to Foucault, it is the threat of surveillance and detection, not the actual detection, that prevents wrongdoing among inmates (1977). In many ways, CCTV attempts to be the modern equivalent of the Panopticon. However, because many incidents involving violence erupt spontaneously, it seems that little can be done to prevent many acts of violence from a surveillance standpoint.

Weapons Control

The existence of weapons in correctional facilities plays a role in violence, particularly severe forms of violence, which may lead to serious injuries and fatalities. Inmates residing in larger facilities are more likely to carry weapons, as are male inmates in comparison with female inmates (Wolff et al. 2007). All prisons prohibit weapons and label them as contraband. However, inmates can smuggle weapons in themselves, or have visitors smuggle them in. Correctional officers and staff have also been known to bring weapons into the facility for the inmates. Far more likely, however, is the creation of weapons from common items, such as toothbrushes, forks, razors, dental floss, magazines, and other frequently distributed items (Atlas 1983b, Hart 2003, Ross 2008).

In order to reduce the potential for weapons in prison, facilities have incorporated preventative approaches into the everyday activities of inmates and correctional staff. For instance, policies such as strip searches of inmates, random searches of individual cells and closer monitoring of visitations all began, in part, to prevent inmates from gaining access to contraband, such as weapons (McShane 2008, Ross 2008). Basic changes to the structure of commonly used items may also prevent these items from being fashioned into weapons. For instance, urethane rubber is now commonly used in toothbrushes, making them more pliable and difficult to use as a stabbing device (Making Corrections Safer 2008).

New Technologies for Violence Prevention

In recent years, prisons have started to utilize technology to prevent violence. For instance, they may implement new technologies to stop inmates from gaining access to weapons. Emulating the technology of backscatter X-rays used in airport security, Graterford State Correctional Institution in Pennsylvania has installed scanners to search visitors. Although they can detect metal objects, even through clothing, these scanners have several drawbacks. They are relatively ineffective at detecting weapons that have been hidden in an individual's body cavities. They are also expensive, large and not portable (Bulman 2009). Despite these drawbacks, officials at Graterford indicate that the scanners have been effective in deterring visitors from attempting to smuggle in contraband, including cell phones and weapons (Whitworth 2010).

Weapons and Non-Permitted Devices Detector (WANDD) devices are smaller, more portable and less expensive. Because of their size, these handheld devices can be used on inmates to detect weapons in their possession, including those that have been smuggled in or those that are handmade (Harne and Scott 2009). They rely on sound waves and are able to detect both metal and nonmetal objects (Bulman 2009).

Another recently introduced technological advance is radio frequency identification (RFID). This mechanism relies on transponders that can be attached to wristbands or other objects that can be worn by inmates. The transponders have sensors to help track inmate movement and also to determine "hot spots" for violence (Bulman 2009). Despite the potential, initial research indicates that RFID is not effective at deterring misconduct and violence among prisoners (Halberstadt and La Vigne 2011). One reason RFID is likely unsuccessful is that inmate violence often erupts spontaneously. Although this technology may be beneficial in helping to understand the time and location of violence, it does little in terms of prevention of violence.

Informal Solutions by Inmates

As previously noted, inmates are not likely to report victimization to correctional staff. While some may join gangs in an attempt to be protected, this is not the only solution. Another option is what Donaldson (2003) refers to as "protective pairing" (306). At first glance, this system seems similar to gang membership; however, protective pairing is an informal agreement between weaker and stronger inmates, in which protection is provided to the weaker in exchange for sexual favors or by performing nonsexual duties for the stronger inmate, such as housekeeping duties (Trammell 2011).

Inmates may also engage in avoidance strategies. For instance, some inmates acknowledge that certain behaviors carry an increased risk of physical and sexual victimization, such as gambling or using drugs. As a result, those risky behaviors may simply be avoided (Ross 2008). Inmates may also avoid certain areas within the prison where they may have an increased fear of victimization. These inmates may limit the amount of time they spend in the showers or the yard, or may choose to stay in their cells and keep to themselves (McCorkle 1992). These isolation strategies have been found to be the most common among victims of physical assault, while those who are sexually victimized are more likely to join a gang for protection (Wolff and Shi 2009).

Inmates as Educators and Leaders

One resource that often goes largely untapped within prisons is the inmates themselves. Newer inmates may benefit from the wisdom and experience of more seasoned inmates. These older or more experienced inmates may serve as positive role models for newly admitted inmates who do not know how to avoid or cope with violence.

An avenue by which inmates may provide insight is through peer-led education programs. Although relatively new to correctional contexts, peer-led education has been successful in reducing physical and sexual violence and increasing awareness among those in traditional educational settings, such as schools and universities (Devilly, Sorbello, Eccleston and Ward 2005). When implemented among inmate populations focusing on violence prevention, participants may exhibit lower levels of confrontation and anger, and greater levels of optimism (Walrath 2001). Peer-led groups have also been used to divert inmates who have been identified as gang members into non-gang lifestyles. Led by former gang members, these groups seek to improve problem-solving skills and provide inmates with alternate means to cope with the difficulties of prison life (Levan 2011).

Inmates may also be used as an intermediary between other inmates and correctional staff. They may serve as gatekeepers to monitor potentially violent situations, or to seek and report characteristics of those who are the most likely to be either perpetrators or victims of physical or sexual violent. These chosen inmates could be specially trained to identify warning signs, specifically focused on vulnerable inmates, such as those who are young, mentally ill or who have been victimized in the community (Sisco and Becker 2007).

Despite the fears that such programs may encourage corruption, violence and intimidation among inmates (DiIulio 1987 and Marquez and Thompson 2006, as cited in Ross 2008), the potential benefits of these initiatives are too great to ignore. Prisoners are often hesitant to confide in correctional treatment staff (Devilly et al. 2005). Coinciding with the "us-versus-them" mentality, treatment staff are often viewed in a similar light as correctional officers. Inmates may be more likely to confide their experiences with violence in other inmates who have endured similar hardships. The peer-leaders themselves will also likely benefit from the experience. They will likely gain a sense of empowerment and responsibility, which will aid in their own rehabilitation and reintegration back into the community (Devilly et al. 2005).

Correctional Officer Training and Intervention

The Correctional Officer Environment

Correctional officers often have taxing jobs. Although they are allowed to leave the confines of the prison at the end of their shift, they spend extended periods of time behind the walls of confinement and in close proximity to the inmates they exert control over. In comparison with other career in criminal justice, they earn relatively low wages (Byrne and Hummer 2008). This, combined with high levels of correctional officer turnover, burnout, stress and long working hours (Schaufeli and Peeters 2000, Lommel 2004), can make their jobs difficult.

Stress among correctional officers has been increasing in recent years. Some factors contributing to these increases include: overcrowding, an increase in the number of inmate on staff assaults, an increase in gang activity and the fact that longer sentences mean that punishments for institutional misconduct (such as increasing the sentence length on an already lengthy prison sentence) have little deterrent effect on the inmates (Finn 2000, 2009).

Issues with correctional officers feeling dissatisfied with their jobs can lead to significant issues within the correctional facility. They may make careless errors, reducing their ability to maintain a safe prison environment (Finn 2009). Some who feel they are underpaid may resort to smuggling weapons, drugs and other contraband in for the inmates in order to earn extra money. The duties of a correctional officer are paramount to ensuring the safety and security of inmates and correctional staff. Attempts to alleviate these many of the existing hardships haven fallen short of their desired effects.

Correctional officers often feel stigmatized and undervalued by the larger society (Liebling 2008), especially in comparison with police officers, who enjoy more respect by their communities. Over time, they become desensitized to violence that occurs among the inmate populations. As they create bonds with each other, they struggle to obtain power within the correctional setting (Liebling 2008). Being vastly outnumbered by the populations they supervise, their means of gaining control include actions such as exerting physical force over individual prisoners (Crawley and Crawley 2008).

Despite many states increasing the minimum salary for correctional officers, there is still difficulty recruiting and retaining qualified officers. Some may view a correctional officer position as a mere stepping stone, and many are unprepared for the stresses involved in a career in corrections. Institutions provide resources for managing stress, such as academy training, in-service training and individual counseling. Many of these initiatives have been criticized for being too generic and not specifically focused on the unique stresses that correctional officers may endure. Moreover, counseling efforts often rely on Employee Assistance Programs, which officers may fear lack confidentiality (Finn 2009).

The Deliberate Indifference Standard

How much responsibility do correctional officers and correctional facilities have in preventing violence? This question was answered in 1994 in the *Farmer v. Brennan* case, which set forth the "deliberate indifference" standard with respect to prison violence. In order for correctional authorities to be found liable, they must 1) be aware that the risk of a serious harm exists and 2) make the inference that such a risk exists (Vaughn and Del Carmen 1995). When writing for the consenting opinion in the *Farmer* case, Justice Souter stated, "Being violently assaulted in prison is simply not part of the penalty that criminal offenders pay for their offenses against society".

Some examples of situations where liability may be found include:

- Leaving cell doors open to aggressors
- Not routinely patrolling locations where violent activities are likely to occur
- Observing an assault in progress and not intervening
- Preventing a victim from escaping a violent situation
  (Vaughn and Del Carmen 1995)

The deliberate indifference standard, however, may not be as easily applied as one might think. Roderick Johnson, a young, nonviolent, African-American, openly homosexual male inmate was set to serve time at Allred Prison in Iowa City, Texas. Upon arrival, he feared that some of his personal characteristics would make him more vulnerable to violence at the hands of his fellow inmates.

Instead of responding appropriately, corrections personnel told Johnson "we don't protect punks on this farm". Johnson was repeatedly brutalized, raped and "sold" by prison gangs over the next 18 months. While Johnson requested transfer to protective custody nine times, prison administrators continually refused his requests, even mocking him by telling him to "learn to fight" or accept that he would continue to be raped (In the Shadows 2006: 15)

In 2005, the court ruled that prison officials were not liable for the violent attacks against Roderick Johnson. This ruling came as a surprise to many, including the ACLU, who had intervened while Mr. Johnson was incarcerated in order to have him transferred to protective custody. As one juror stated, "He probably was (raped), but he never came out with a rape test" (Brown 2005). For many, this case set a precedent in terms of the amount of proof required in order to prevail in a case of deliberate indifference with respect to prison violence.

The Prison Rape Elimination Act

In response to the flawed data previously recorded, as well as high profile cases, such as Roderick Johnson's case, the Prison Rape Elimination Act (PREA) was passed in 2003. This provides funding, information, resources and recommendations to federal, state and local correctional facilities in an attempt to illuminate and possibly reduce the problem. The major provisions of the PREA include:

- Developing mechanisms to detect, prevent, reduce and punish incidents of prison rape
- Collecting and disseminating information related to prison rape
- Implementing and adhering to zero tolerance policies for prison rape
- Awarding financial assistance to help correctional governments and facilities achieve these goals

Over 7,600 correctional facilities are currently included in the annual report, which is compiled by the Bureau of Justice Statistics and provided to the Attorney General. In 2008, adult facilities reported 7,444 allegations of sexual victimization (Beck 2011). This number presents an interesting picture, especially considering that just a few decades ago, sexual victimization in prison was a topic that was considered practically nonexistent.

Ultimately, the PREA is a step towards accountability. Rates are compared across facilities so that those institutions with higher rates of sexual assault not only must explain why their facility has higher rates, but also take steps to correct the issue. Government funding is also tied to PREA compliance. The resulting effect is that data collection on rape has become prioritized in an effort to change the attitudes of correctional administrators and make it more of a pressing issue (Corlew 2006).

Conclusion

In recognition of the prevailing problem, much has been done to try to reduce prison violence. Some solutions may be implemented on a government level, while others are implemented at the facility level. When these solutions fall short in solving the problem, inmates may seek their own informal solutions. These solutions may lead to more dissention and violence. As such, it seems sensible to consider what other solutions should be considered that may be more effective at reducing prison violence.

Chapter 8

The Long Road Ahead:
The Future of Prison Violence

Introduction

In a policy-based article, Mears (2008) argues that prison violence can be explained and understood by examining a set of interrelated factors. These include a lack of programming that fulfills inmate needs (Petersilia 2003), proliferation of gangs (Grann 2004, Griffin 2007), constant major shifts or changes in prison administration (Riveland 1999) and inmates who have issues with mental health and substance abuse (Mears 2004). This explanation provides excellent insight as to the complexities of the issue as well as sets forth potential solutions to the problem.

As has been described in the preceding chapters, prison violence is an issue with which people should be concerned. It is very difficult to know exactly how great the scope of this problem is, and the extent of the problem varies geographically, not only on a macro level (by nation and state), but also on a micro level (within individual facilities). There are many potential solutions to reducing the prevalence of violence among prisoners, some of which have already been implemented.

In a 2005 article, Edgar discusses three different approaches to responding to prison violence. The first is inmate-centered, and can be accomplished in ways such as providing an inmate's basic needs or by making sure the facility provides a safe haven for the inmate population. Secondly, the inmates may be allowed their own personal autonomy, which discourages violence. Autonomy could be accomplished by simply allowing the inmates the freedom to attend the appropriate optional programming, or allowing them to make purchases at the canteen. The final approach focuses on implementation of restorative justice panels that handle conflicts among the inmate populations in a nonviolent manner (Byrne, Hummer and Stowell 2008). The bulk of the approaches currently used can be classified under the inmate-level approach. However, more initiatives need to be implemented to appropriately reduce the incidence of violence. More importantly, prevention of violence needs to be more proactive, rather than reactive.

Segregation Policies

As stated in previous chapters, the evidence of potential damage done to inmates who are segregated from the general population is universal. Despite the concerns over the emotional damage to inmates who are placed in solitary confinement, the rate of confinement for segregated inmates has increased at a more rapid pace than that of the general prison population. Between 1995 and 2000, this equated to a 40 percent increase (Gibbons 2011). It makes one wonder why a practice that has been shown to be damaging, as well as being twice as expensive, would continue to be a fairly commonly accepted practice.

Many inmates are placed in more segregated housing as a result of engaging in violence against other inmates. This is meant as a punishment and perhaps as a deterrence mechanism. But this response seems highly ineffective when considering the cycle of violence that perpetuates among inmates. Today's victim is often tomorrow's assailant, and vice versa (Edgar, O'Donnell and Martin 2003). This punitive measure seems to ignore this potential cycle.

There have been several recent recommendations for changes in the use of segregation and solitary confinement. First, segregation should be used as a last resort, and should be truly reserved for those who are the worst offenders behind bars and who have committed the most violent infractions (Gibbons 2011). Many have condemned the current segregation policies as being overly used. Segregation is not a deterrent to inmate behavior, either from a specific or a general deterrence standpoint. Violence often erupts spontaneously, giving assailants little to no time to rationally consider the consequences of their actions. Upon returning to the general population, it is doubtful that they will be specifically deterred from continuing to commit violence against their fellow inmates or correctional staff for this same reason. In fact, if abiding by the tenets of the convict code, solitary confinement would in fact prompt inmates to engage in vigilante justice, which means that it actually leads to an *increase* in violence among inmates.

Those who are placed in solitary confinement are currently stripped of any human contact. This includes the loss of any family visitation time, education, vocational training or treatment. Although these privileges may be returned to the inmate upon their return to the general prison population, whatever time is spent in isolation is destined to be monotonous, devoid of all human contact, and preventing any aspirations of rehabilitation or reform. Allowing inmates to continue to participate in whatever programming that they were participating in prior to their segregation would have multiple benefits (Gibbons 2011). Not only would it potentially prevent the negative effects of isolation, but it would also not cause a disruption in whatever rehabilitation efforts were already begun.

Finally, inmates who suffer with a mental illness are often placed in solitary confinement because correctional administrators and officers simply do not know how to react to their behavior. Mental illness may be acted out in ways that not only violate the norms and values of the prison culture, but also in ways that violate the correctional facilities set of policies. The effects of solitary confinement can be even more damaging to an inmate with preexisting mental health conditions. Thus, mentally ill inmates should be handled separately from those without a mental illness, and be placed in therapeutic environments that are separate from the rest of the facility (Gibbons 2011).

Treatment Options

Treatment and rehabilitation programs are far better solutions to dealing with the bulk of the offender population than imprisonment. It has been estimated that spending $1 million on treatment will reduce crime 15 times more effectively than incapacitation (Mauer 2006a). Providing treatment, as well as actively promoting inmate participation in it, is one recommendation to preventing misconduct and violence among prisoners (Gibbons 2011).

Focusing treatment efforts on those who are likely to be involved in violence, either as a victim or as an offender, can help streamline programs, control costs and improve effectiveness. Most prisons offer some form of psychological treatment for those identified as violent. For instance, anger management may be offered but is generally restricted to those who are violent offenders, or to those who commit violence while incarcerated (Vannoy and Hoyt 2004). Appropriate treatment programs can help prevent commission of violence upon release, including sexual offenses and domestic violence offenses (MacKenzie 2006, Bobbitt, Campbell and Tate 2011). These programs likely also help prevent violence while incarcerated.

One type of therapy that has been shown to be effective is cognitive behavioral therapy (CBT). CBT may be particularly effective in preventing sexual violence. This type of treatment is based on the belief that individuals can consciously alter their behavior and specifically monitor themselves for warning signs of a relapse (MacKenzie 2006). It also focuses on replacing deviant behaviors with more prosocial behaviors. CBT has been shown to be more effective when it 1) includes problem solving and anger management skills, 2) uses quality training coupled with close monitoring of subjects and 3) is used on those who have the greatest risk (Lipsey, Landenberger and Wilson 2007).

Although CBT has shown success in reducing the likelihood of recidivism upon release, it is something that should be considered for all inmates in an effort to reduce violence while incarcerated. The convict code and inmate culture have historically valued deviant and antisocial behavior. Providing CBT to all inmates would likely negate this environment, potentially helping to disentangle the convict code and provide a safer environment for all. Doing this would allow prison administrators to focus on segregating the hypothetically few inmates who do not respond to CBT and continue to behave violently, while allowing those who do respond positively to remain among the general inmate population.

Educational and Vocational Opportunities

Recent decades have seen a dramatic decrease in the opportunities afforded to inmates to increase their education and employment training. Inmates enter correctional facilities with less formal education than their law-abiding counterparts, with more than 40 percent having not completed high school (Harlow

2003). Similarly, many inmates do not have marketable job skills upon entering prison (Andrews and Bonta 2003).

The existing literature examining the link between vocational and educational opportunities and the likelihood of recidivism is vast. The bulk of this research indicates that inmates who participate in these programs are more likely to successfully reintegrate into the community upon their release (Schumaker, Anderson and Anderson 1990, Petersilia 2003, Byrne and Hummer 2008, Ross 2008, Rose, Reschenberg and Richards 2010, Gibbons 2011). Not only do these efforts provide increased employment and opportunities for secondary education, but they also promote a positive self-image, help build prosocial bonds and encourage discipline among participants.

Aside from these benefits, increased educational and vocational opportunities in facilities coincide with fewer incidents of violence among inmates (McCorkle et al. 1995, Ward 2009, Perez et al. 2010). Reductions in violence may result from the same processes that allow for successful community reintegration promoting positive self-image, helping to build prosocial bonds and encouraging discipline. It may also be that participation in these programs allow for less free time, decreasing the opportunities for violence. One observation made is that as the prison population continues to increase, there are fewer opportunities for education and vocational training (Hassine 2010). Those who are the most psychologically damaged from prison are those who are unable to participate in meaningful activities, such as education or vocational training (McCorkle 1993). As such, it seems imperative that regardless of the fluctuations in the prison population, ample opportunities for education and work should continue to be available to inmates. Moreover, the correctional system should provide more incentives for inmates to participate in both educational and vocational programs. Assisting participating inmates with finding and securing employment upon their release would encourage inmates to participate in these programs (Trammell 2012). Those who are working to reintegrate into the community are less likely to engage in violence if they are actively working or being trained, or if they are working toward an education (Ullrich and Coid 2011).

Cultural Diversity Awareness

Inmates who become entrenched in the prison culture may begin to have tunnel vision, focusing on what is in the best interest for those of their own race or ethnicity. This focus often begins with, and is continuously reinforced by, gang membership and racial segregation. As discussed throughout this book, gangs and racial tension guide the existing prison culture. Even though official racial segregation has been declared unconstitutional, facilities may still segregate if there is a compelling interest to do so. Facilities that are not officially segregated by prison administrators are unofficially and informally segregated by the inmates. Visits to prisons reveal that inmates informally racially segregate common areas, such as the cafeteria, day room and recreation area. On an individual level, most inmates refuse to have a cellmate from a different race, and forced racial desegregation has been blamed for inciting prison riots (Wilkinson and Unwin 1999, Trammell 2012). Many inmates are from neighborhoods where they have little to no exposure to individuals belonging to other races, ethnicities or cultures, especially considering that many of these neighborhoods also have informal racial and ethnic segregation.

How can we increase the tolerance and acceptance of other cultures and backgrounds? Rebecca Trammell (2012) suggests introducing cultural diversity programs and multicultural activities. These programs and activities could expose inmates to unique perspectives and insights, different from their own. Doing so promotes tolerance and may prevent inmates from informally segregating themselves and from joining gangs that reinforce their own racial or ethnic singularity. Ultimately, this would likely lead to less racial tension and violence.

Strengthening Familial Bonds and Relationships

Another recommendation to reducing inmate violence is to allow inmates to maintain, and even strengthen, their ties with their family members. These bonds have been linked with both reducing recidivism upon release and reducing violence while incarcerated (Wilczak and Markstrom 1999, Casey-Acevedo and Bakken 2001, Tewksbury and DeMichele 2001, Petersilia 2003, Bales and Mears 2008). Separation from loved ones has been linked to increased levels of stress (Bobbitt et al. 2011), which could potentially increase violent tendencies. One way in which family ties can reduce misbehavior is by increasing the opportunities for family visitation privileges. Inmates engaging in violence risk having these privileges revoked (Carlson and Garrett 2008).

The relationship between behavior and visitation is more complex than this. Visitation allows inmates to maintain prosocial bonds, even in an environment that predominantly encourages behaviors and attitudes that counters these attitudes. Not only do the inmates have the opportunities to briefly interact with their families, they also look forward to their release date so they can be reunited with their family members. Family visits are also correlated with inmates having arranged living accommodations and employment upon their release (Codd 2008), which could lead to lower recidivism rates in the community.

Inmate families also may reap the benefits of visitation with their loved one. Being able to see their incarcerated parent allows for children to see that they are adjusting to prison and that they are not harmed (Landreth and Lobaugh 1998). It can also reduce the feelings of loss that accompany parental incarceration (Johnston 1995). Beyond the prison walls, positive results are seen as well. Maintaining strong family ties has been closely associated with a lower prevalence of delinquency (Bilchik 2007). Most importantly, many children indicate that they want the ability to visit with their incarcerated parent (Hairston 2001).

Despite the benefits, there are many barriers to family visitation and communication that must be reduced or eliminated. The distance between the correctional facility and the inmate's family is a major obstacle. Not only do many families have to travel more than 100 miles to visit their incarcerated family member (Casey and Wiatrowski 1996), but they also often do not have the transportation necessary to do so (Petersilia 2003). Once at the facility, families often find the environment unwelcoming to visitors (Gibbons 2011). Overly strict regulations on visitation often make visitors feel stigmatized or degraded, resulting in a decline in the frequency of visits over time (Comfort 2003, Arditti 2005).

In order to increase the bonds between inmates and families, it is necessary to reexamine where prisons are located (Gibbons 2011). More careful consideration should be given to which facility an inmate will be housed in, specifically allowing them to be as close to their families as possible. If it is necessary to house inmates and their families great distances apart, perhaps special accommodations could be made to provide transportation to those family members. Additionally, making visitation areas more welcoming for children would also be helpful (Gibbons 2011). For example, play areas could be added to waiting rooms of visitation areas, as many families wait for extended periods of time (Sturges 2002).

If these changes are not enough to allow for increased visitation, another solution may be to increase the use of technology to allow for communication. More and more facilities are using various forms of video visitation (Arditti 2005). This allows families to remain in contact with the incarcerated person, even if they cannot physically be in the same location. It also prevents children and spouses from any potentially negative effects of the waiting rooms or visitation areas of the prisons.

Upon release from prison, maintaining bonds with noncriminogenic family and friends remains paramount to preventing crime and violence. Of the five factors identified as protective against violence commission among released prisoners, three of these involve prosocial bonds with family and friends. Systems for emotional support, social support, and spending time with family and friends have all been found to be positively correlated with desisting from violence (Ullrich and Coid 2011). It seems highly pertinent, then, to ensure that these bonds remain strong as former inmates work to be reintegrated into the community.

Gang Diversion Programs

In order to reduce the level of gang involvement among inmates, some researchers advocate that potential members are diverted from gangs prior to their arrival at prison. Some inmates import their gang affiliation into the facility from the community. The estimated percentage of jail inmates who are affiliated with a gang is about 20 percent. It has been hypothesized that the best way to prevent future prisoners from joining gangs is to focus on the jail populations, since many of these inmates will ultimately be released, only to be later incarcerated in prisons (Ruddell et al. 2006).

Two major goals may be accomplished by focusing on gang membership at the jail level. First, if jail inmates can be diverted from gangs, they may be more likely to adopt prosocial attitudes and desist from crime. This means they may be returned to the community and, with the appropriate treatment and supervision, not commit future offenses. If they do continue to offend and ultimately become housed in prison, they are not entering as an existing gang member. At the prison level, they may be able to avoid gang membership if the prison administration takes a proactive role in discouraging gang membership.

National Crime Victimization Survey (NCVS) Equivalency

On the community level, policy makers and criminal justice practitioners have long acknowledged the flaws that are inherent to official crime reporting mechanisms. The National Incident Based Reporting System (NIBRS) and the Uniform Crime Report (UCR), which inform national crime statistics, are fraught with errors. The most blatant issue is that these measurement tools only include reported crimes. Roughly half of all crimes that are committed in the community are not reported to the police. This percentage varies and is dependent on many factors, including the type of offense and the victim–offender relationship.

In order to help rectify some of these issues, the community has also been provided with the National Crime Victimization Survey (NCVS). Rather than focusing solely on incidents brought to the attention of the police, the NCVS allows for a representative sample of individuals to be surveyed about their victimization experiences. While it is far from a perfect measure of crime, the NCVS does allow for capturing what has been termed "the dark figure of crime", or that which is undetected and unreported to law enforcement.

In light of the issues raised in previous chapters regarding inmates being reluctant to report their victimization experiences, it makes little sense for us to continue to use official correctional disciplinary reports and records to inform our prison policies. Inmates seem more willing to disclose their victimization to third parties, such as researchers, especially if their anonymity or confidentiality is assured. Implementing an NCVS-style instrument would allow those who are embarrassed, afraid or dismissive of their experiences to unofficially report them. This alleviates many of the issues associated with official reporting. Victims would be less likely to fear vigilante justice from the perpetrator, and they would also be less concerned with being placed in protective custody. Although there may be initial feelings of shame or embarrassment, they would be less likely to have to contend with official labeling by other inmates (with the exception of those who already were aware of the assault). They also would not have to deal with correctional officer issues, such as a fear of no action being taken against the perpetrator, or the fear of not being believed.

Victimization-style reporting can also be helpful in that it can assist in informing correctional officers, wardens and policy makers in order to reduce the frequency of future victimization. In-depth questions can be asked regarding the circumstances of the crime, such as the location, nature of the offense, victim–offender relationship and whether any injuries were sustained. This style of measurement is a marked improvement over the existing reporting system in a number of ways.

Restorative Justice Panels

Implementation of restorative justice panels has proven to be successful in the community to help resolve differences between assailants and victims. In recent years, the criminal justice system has been criticized for reducing the voice of the victim, and restorative justice provides victims with more of a voice. Punishment-oriented philosophies are naturally designed to focus on the offender, rather than on the harms done to the victim and the community. A prominent vehicle in the modern criminal justice system to achieve restorative justice is through victim–offender mediation panels. These panels encourage healing. Not only are victims provided the opportunity to explain the damages done by the offenders, but the offenders are also able to connect their actions with the consequences of those actions. In short, restorative justice is premised on crime being a violation of relationships among individuals, rather than simply as a violation of the law (Latimer, Dowden and Muise 2005). Although the bulk of restorative justice research has focused on property crimes, the few studies that have examined the results for violent offenses show promising results. Victims of violence indicate that restorative justice efforts provide them with closure, relief and feelings of gratitude for having the opportunity to be given a voice in their own victimization experiences (Umbreit, Coates and Vos 2006).

Despite the increasing role of restorative justice in the community, such panels are not commonly used in correctional settings. Restorative justice allows prisons "to create a more harmonious environment for prisoners, their families and for staff and management" (Newell 2002: 1, as cited in Dhami, Mantle and Fox 2009). Restorative justice panels are a way for inmates to resolve their differences peacefully, without disciplinary involvement from correctional administrators, and for them to be held personally accountable for their actions (Guidoni 2003, Edgar 2008, Byrne, Hummer and Stowell 2008). They can also help improve prosocial skills and increase an inmate's self-esteem. In addition to these benefits, which are similar to those found in restorative justice efforts found in the community, there is an additional major benefit to programs used in correctional settings. Restorative justice panels may improve on the relationships between inmates and correctional staff. In order to mediate panels, correctional staff must develop specialized skills, ultimately improving their communication skills with inmates and allowing them to gain insight into their unique experiences (Dhami et al. 2009).

A few countries have begun to use restorative justice efforts and victim–offender mediation panels in prisons. Two nations that have used some form of restorative justice model for these purposes are the United Kingdom and Belgium (Hagemann 2008). Most of the restorative justice efforts are focused on the crimes that the offender committed prior to their incarceration, and often involves the victims coming to the prison to confront the inmate (Biermans and D'Hoop 2001). These efforts are certainly a step in the right direction, but the scope should be broadened so that similar panels are used to address violence that occurs among inmates as part of their incarceration experience. Prisoners who have friendships or relationships with each other are more likely to resort to nonviolent conflict resolution (Edgar et al. 2003). Thus, it seems that panels, which encourage communication and maintaining or building relationships among inmates, would be beneficial in reducing and responding to violence.

Medical Care

Prisons have infirmaries and medical staff to treat inmates when they are ill or injured. Victims of physical and sexual violence may sustain injuries or contract diseases as a result of these victimizations. As established in *Estelle v. Gamble*, inmates are guaranteed medical care by the Eighth Amendment. Although they are guaranteed medical care the quality of this care may be left to interpretation. The guideline generally applied is the principle of least eligibility. This concept states that inmates should only be provided with access to equal levels of services available to those who are noncriminogenic and living in the free community (Feest 1999). Correctional policies are sometimes criticized as viewing and treating inmates as "less deserving of the most basic amenities and civilities, and ultimately less than human" (King 1998: 617, as quoted in Dabney and Vaughn 2000).

Illustrative of these issues are the extent and results of inmate lawsuits regarding the quality of medical care received while they are incarcerated. In their study of inmate lawsuits, Dabney and Vaughn (2000) found that half of the cases alleged poor or improper care, and 20 percent involved denial of medical care. The results of the allegations are also profound, ranging from a temporary loss in the quality of life to death. Specific examples provided in this study include amputations as a result of gangrene, blindness and enduring seven months of untreated tuberculosis.

As horrific as these results are, there are undoubtedly more examples that have gone unreported. It is questionable whether some facilities are adhering to the principle of least eligibility. Even assuming that they are, it should be taken into consideration that inmates are routinely subjected to physical and sexual abuse far worse than many in the general community. If institutions are unable to prevent these atrocities from occurring, they should, at a minimum, provide the appropriate medical care to the victims.

Garbage In, Violence Out?

Personal visits to state prisons have revealed the daily cost of meals to be between $2 and $3 per inmate. In most states, this includes three meals per day. In Georgia, state prisoners receive two meals per day on Fridays, Saturdays and Sundays; state prisoners in Arizona, Ohio and Texas receive two meals per day on Saturdays and Sundays. This means the length of time between meals can sometimes be quite substantial. For instance, on the weekends, Texas state inmates eat their first meal between 5:00 a,m, and 7:00 a.m., and their second meal is consumed between 4:00 p.m. and 6:30 p.m. (Fernandez 2011).

Anyone who has visited a grocery store and prepared his or her own meals understands the cost of food. While the quality of prison food varies greatly between facilities, spending up to $3 per day for between two and three meals likely does not equate to high-quality cuisine. Prison menus are often viewed as deserved additional punishment by the public. Even publication of an inmate's last meal request prior to their execution can incite anger among the public.

What should be considered are the potential effects of diet on inmate behavior. The link between the quality of nutrition and individual behavior in the community has been well documented and studied. Little interest or research has been directed at understanding the effects of improper nutrition among inmates, but it seems logical to assume poor nutrition could result in increased levels of aggression and violence among prison populations. In addition to long periods between meals and inadequate food, there is also concern that after preparation, food sits idly by for as long as 45 minutes, causing it to lose whatever nutritional content it may have originally had (Serving Time 2006).

Recent studies have examined the effects of nutritional supplements. Comparing inmates who are provided with supplements with those in the control group who are given placebos indicate marked differences. Those given supplements display fewer tendencies toward antisocial behavior and a significant reduction in the number of violent acts perpetrated (Serving Time 2006, Bohannon 2009).

The links between diet, nutrition and violence are certainly worth further exploration. In an environment where correctional facilities are striving to cut costs, reducing the number of meals or quality of food may be to the detriment of the prison environment. Trying to save money on food could potentially be more costly, if malnourished inmates are more likely to be violent and aggressive.

Correctional Officer Culture

There is no denying that correctional officers play an integral role in the prison culture. Some participate in prison violence, either directly or indirectly. Directly, the officers that are the most entrenched in the prison culture may commit violent acts themselves. They may also indirectly engage in violence by being deliberately indifferent to inmate violence. Some examples may include intentionally leaving inmates' cell doors unlocked or open, or not intervening when an assault is in progress. At the very core of the adversarial relationship between officers and inmates lies conflict and competing roles in the prison culture.

Correctional officer training is at the heart of the issue (Wolff and Shi 2009). One change that has been predicted to have an effect is to reduce the use of physical force and weaponry, reserving it for cases that are deemed absolutely necessary (Gibbons 2011). As learning theory posits, when individuals continue to be exposed to violence, they become more desensitized to it. Although many of the inmates herald from community backgrounds that may have predisposed them to violence, continual exposure can exacerbate the effects. Furthermore, in an environment plagued by vigilante justice as a plausible and acceptable resolution, the use of physical force can have obvious and profound effects.

Specialized and specific training is also needed to assist correctional staff in recognizing when violence is occurring. With so many incidents going unreported, correctional officers often have little direct exposure to particular types of violence, especially sexual violence. Most of their knowledge is derived from secondhand accounts, reading official reports or informal discussions with other correctional staff (Owen and Wells 2006). Furthermore, they may view assaultive behavior as deserved, or have difficulty knowing whether activities are forced or consensual (Eigenberg 1989, 2000, Hensley and Tewksbury 2005, Owen and Wells 2006, Owen et al. 2007). This combination of potential factors means that officers may be either unwilling or unsure whether intervention is necessary or appropriate in particular situations.

To improve upon the existing training provided to correctional officers, there should be more emphasis placed on identifying and responding to violence. Even more important than this aspect may be sensitivity training. Many police departments mandate that their officers undergo training to understand and provide empathy to victims. Similar courses should be required of correctional officers so that they can acknowledge and respond to violent victimization appropriately. Moreover, this training should be longitudinal, perhaps provided annually to prevent the development of a culture among correctional officers that either dismisses or condones prison violence.

Changing the Degree of Social Distance

One of the side effects of the increasing prison population and overcrowding of the correctional facilities is the increase in social distance between correctional staff and inmates (Liebling 2008). Hassine (2010) describes social distance as the degree of familiarity between groups. When examining correctional institutions, social distance can be examined by the relationships between correctional officers and inmates, treatment staff and inmates, and correctional officers and treatment staff.

Social distance between correctional officers and inmates is partially determined by the ratio of security staff to inmates, as well as the amount of contact between these two groups (Hassine 2010). In comparison with other countries, the United States has a higher staff to inmate ratio, often as high as 100:1 (Byrne and Hummer 2008). It is therefore expected that the social distance between inmates and correctional officers is greater in the United States than in many other nations. As control of the inmate population becomes more important, the well-being and treatment of inmates becomes less critical to the correctional officers, and perhaps to the correctional facility as a whole (Fagan 2003, as cited in Lurigio and Snowden 2008). Social distance can also be created or increased if correctional officers distrust prisoners (Crouch and Marquart 1980, as cited in Liebling 2008), a condition also endemic to the American prison system, as dictated by prison culture. Personal interaction between inmates and security staff thus becomes more managerial and formal and less individualized and frequent (Byrne and Hummer 2008).

In contrast, the degree of social distance between treatment staff and inmates is generally determined by how much emphasis is placed on rehabilitation efforts at the facility level (Hassine 2010). This emphasis often varies based on facility characteristics. For instance, it is expected that smaller, lower security-level institutions would focus more on rehabilitation efforts than institutions that are larger and of a higher security levels.

Finally, the relationship between treatment staff and security staff is one that may be inherently strained. The roles of these two groups, especially in larger, more impersonal correctional facilities, focus on opposing goals of punishment. Whereas treatment staff often primarily focuses on rehabilitation and eventual reintegration into the community, correctional officers' primary focuses are on order maintenance, security and control (Liebling 2008). The degree of social distance between these two groups is partially determined by the type of facility and whether the institution's primary focus is on rehabilitation and treatment, or on the control of an inmate population that may be viewed as virtually uncontrollable. It may also be determined by the individual characteristics of the staff members themselves, whose personal views of correctional goals are likely reflected in their interactions with other groups.

In terms of preventing violence, it may seem that increasing the social distance between inmates and security staff is the most beneficial, as this allows for more control to be exerted over the prisoners. It may well serve both security and treatment staff to be personally invested in the well-being of the inmates. Although order maintenance of prisons should not be abandoned, security staff should express concern and humanity for those they control. Furthermore, since a lack of trust has been cited as a primary reason for inmates to not report victimization (Edgar, O'Donnell and Martin 2003), decreasing the social distance will likely encourage reporting of incidents that occur. By correctional staff ensuring that inmates participate in various programs and treatment efforts, and effectively communicating their concern for these inmates, the prisoners may be more likely to feel attached and to be interested in building prosocial bonds.

Softening the "Tough on Crime" Approach

As discussed in Chapter 3, overcrowding in prisons is an issue that many countries seem to be facing. Housing too many individuals in a particular space can lead to stress and frustration. Overcrowding is perhaps one of the greatest and most well cited contributors to prison violence (Gibbons 2011). The likelihood of violent victimization increases as inmates are housed two or three to a cell originally designed to house one person. In some circumstances, many inmates may be housed in a dormitory-style setting, with gymnasiums or day rooms being converted into housing units holding multiple bunk beds. Because a great deal of violence has been cited to occur among cellmates or inmates housed together, multiple housing units are breeding grounds for victimization.

It would then seem that the most straightforward approach that could have the greatest effect on reducing prison violence is a move toward decarceration (Austin and Irwin 2012). Many may fear that this movement could result in a significant increase in crime. For many years, the public has followed governmental pushes toward a "get tough on crime" approach, believing that locking criminals away for long periods of time would subsequently reduce crime. After all, it seems logical to believe that once someone is incapacitated, they can no longer commit crimes against the public.

However, the reality is that high incarceration rates may ultimately lead to an increase in crime, although there may be a time lag before this increase is experienced. Consider the many inmates who are currently serving long sentences (perhaps 20 years or more) for nonviolent offenses. If prisons are indeed "schools of crime", as posited by the importation theory, inmates are likely becoming more criminogenic as a result of their incarceration experiences. Those who are released in the future who committed a nonviolent offense are likely returning to their communities more criminogenic (and perhaps more violent) than they were upon entering the prison system. Couple this with the significant disadvantages they will continue to face upon their release (lack of employment, civic disengagement, broken familial bonds, etc.), and there is little doubt that these individuals will recidivate.

Of course, it does not make sense to eliminate prison completely. A lack of correctional facilities could signal a return to the extreme corporal and capital punishments of the Hammurabi Code. Prison sanctions remain sensible sentences for violent offenders, especially repeat violent offenders. Those who are more likely candidates for alternative sanctions are those who commit nonviolent offenses, such as drug and property crimes. The single greatest decrease in reducing the prison population would come from decriminalizing drugs. This could lower the size of the prison population by at least 25 percent (Jacobs 2007). It should be noted that decriminalization does not mean legalization of drugs. Rather, this is an approach that would decrease the penalties for drug offenses to a fine, probation, mandatory rehabilitation program or some other sanction that does not involve incarceration. Simply providing those with a substance abuse problem the tools for rehabilitation in the community, rather than subjecting them to the further abuses of incarceration, would reduce the likelihood of their future involvement in criminal activity.

Similarly, diversion programs could be used more frequently for particular types of offenders. For example, those who commit simple assaults could be diverted to an anger management program, or those who commit sex offenses (especially those that are not aggravated offenses, such as statutory rape), could be sanctioned to sex therapy sessions (Jacobs 2007).

Increasing the use of probation and suspended sentences would have a significant effect on the incarceration rate, and would also save a significant amount of money. This means that more focus and money would need to be invested in probation services (Jacobs 2007, Austin and Irwin 2012). For instance, more probation officers would need to be hired in order to keep their caseloads relatively low, allowing for more supervision of their clients. A shift in sentencing practices must be accompanied with a shift in resources. In order to satiate the public, there must also be evidence that decreasing the incarceration of offenders does not lead to a subsequent increase in crime, and should, in fact, show a decrease in crime.

By reducing the prison population, violence can be decreased in a few ways. With fewer individuals behind bars, there are fewer opportunities for violence. Alleviating overcrowding would ultimately prevent dormitory-style housing, which is a leading contributor to the issue. By only imprisoning those who are deemed the most criminogenic and who pose the greatest threat to the community, we are essentially eliminating the population that is the most vulnerable to being violently victimized in prison: nonviolent offenders. Once this population has been removed, more focus can be placed on rehabilitating the violent populations that remain incarcerated in the hope of many of them eventually returning to society.

Public Knowledge, Awareness and Institutional Accountability

Educating the public on the large-scale harms prison threatens to the prisoner, their family, community and society is of utmost importance. Politicians and policy makers must be able to honestly engage in dialogue with their constituents on crime and its consequences. Ultimately, "we need to create an environment that allows policy makers to support rational policy and to not be fearful that doing so will harm their political careers" (Mauer 2011: 702).

One of the recommendations repeatedly mentioned in the literature as necessary to reducing prison violence is holding correctional institutions accountable. The Prison Rape Elimination Act (PREA) is one way that facilities are currently being held accountable (Corlew 2006). Accountability under the PREA is limited to sexually violent incidents. But, shouldn't they be held accountable whenever an inmate is subjected to any type of violence? When inmates leave prison and are reintegrated to their respective communities, they are generally placed on parole as a mechanism by which they can be monitored. Recidivism is seen as a failure on their part, and society holds them accountable for these failures by either increasing their parole restrictions or returning them to prison.

But, has the correctional system failed these individuals, as well as their families, communities and society, by returning people who have not been rehabilitated to the streets? Worse yet, has the system contributed even more to the problem by exposing them to daily doses of violence that they are likely unable to escape from? Is the criminal justice system setting people up to fail?

Although inmates should be liable for their own behavior, the system is certainly not without blame. Society has come to expect that they can hold other institutions, such as schools and law-enforcement agencies, accountable when they fail to provide the services that they are intended and designed to provide. Nationally standardized benchmarks are needed to know whether our correctional facilities are effectively rehabilitating inmates and preventing exposure to violence (Byrne, Hummer and Stowell 2008, Wolff and Shi 2009). The only way for correctional administrators to be held accountable is if prisons are no longer considered a vacuum within society. The events occurring behind the walls and bars must be made public, and must be widely disseminated and publicized (Wolff and Shi 2009), as has become customary in other countries, such as Scotland (Fairweather 2002). What happens in prison doesn't stay in prison; it returns to the community. Citizens have the right and the responsibility to hold the criminal justice system accountable when other members of society have been failed by their efforts.

Research

The lack of quality research that has been conducted contributes greatly to the lack of understanding of how to best alleviate the issues associated with prison violence. As Byrne, Hummer and Stowell (2008) indicate "We don't know 'what works' in prisons and jails because the necessary evaluation research (independent, external, and using randomized designs) has yet to be completed" (206). In particular, despite decades of research on prisons, prisoners and the prison culture, we lack information about the circumstances of the events that lead to violent incidents (Edgar 2008). Reliable and valid data is crucial to understanding the extent of victimization, as well as helping to prevent violence from occurring (Wolff, Shi and Bachman 2008).

Additionally, there is scant research on the effects of violence on prisoners. Though a growing body of research is beginning to emerge on sexual violence, inarguably one of the most severe forms of violence that can be experienced, there is an absence of research on how other forms of violence, such as threats, fighting and minor physical assaults, may influence the individual and the experiences that they have upon returning to their community. The Prison Rape Elimination Act will undoubtedly continue to raise awareness and interest in research and education on sexual violence. Although sexual violence is certainly worthy of study, many more inmates are exposed to lesser forms of violence, either as direct victims or as witnesses.

Similar legislation would need to be passed in order to raise awareness on the effects and dangers of all forms of violence perpetrated behind bars. This exposure can have lasting effects on individuals, and because these transactions commonly occur, it is extremely important that their effects are clearly understood. Just as the PREA seeks to increase the knowledge of prison rape incidents, there should be similar efforts to provide research, data collection and accountability for all forms of prison violence. All violence has negative consequences, and although a zero-tolerance policy has been adopted for prison rape, it must be taken for all forms of prison violence.

Moreover, additional policy-based research is needed to examine the macro level effects of laws (Mauer 2011). Passing more laws often equates to incarcerating more individuals, and astronomical correctional costs. These costs are not only financial, but social costs as well. Incarceration affects many aspects of society, from family structures to unemployment rates. More investigation must be completed to understand the full effects that mass incarceration has on society.

Conclusion: Ready or Not, Here They Come

At year-end 2010, the United States released more inmates from prison than they admitted to prisons, totaling 708,667 and 703,798, respectively (Guerino et al. 2011). This is the first time this event has occurred in decades. Is this a random occurrence? Or does this represent the beginning of a shift in how the nation views punishment and sentencing?

Perhaps this change means the revolving door of prison is finally beginning to slow down. I would like to take the optimistic perspective and believe that someone is paying attention and is beginning to declare that the approach we have taken to punishment over the past few decades is simply ineffective. As Nelken (2011) poignantly observes, prison rates are not just a product of crime rates and sentencing, but also a "product of reflective responses by politicians and policy makers to their perceptions of where their countries stand in relation to other places" (107).

The total number of parolees in 2010 exceeded 840,000 (Glaze and Bonczar 2011). This means that there are hundreds of thousands of individuals trying to readapt and reintegrate into society, most of who have been exposed to a world of violence, some for long periods of time. The question is whether or not they are ready. Only slightly more than half of parolees successfully complete the terms of their probation, and over a third of parolees are reincarcerated, due to their parole being revoked or receiving a new prison sentence (Glaze and Bonczar 2011). Even those who do successfully complete their parole may still eventually reoffend and become incarcerated again.

Our current system is not correcting anyone. In fact, it is making individuals, communities and society at large more criminogenic and violent. Continuing incarceration at the rate we have, with no revisions to how we handle treatment and programming, seems foolish. As a civilized society, it seems our duty and obligation that we value the worth of every individual, at least enough to allow them to be healed and rehabilitated while they serve out their prescribed sentences. Putting more and more people behind bars, and subjecting them to a daily dose of violence, will accomplish nothing positive for our society. Allowing them to return to their families and communities to be productive members of society will.

Fyodor Dostoevsky once wrote, "The degree of civilization in a society is revealed by entering its prisons". Upon entering prisons, there is little doubt that the average visitor feels anxious and unsafe in an environment filled with fear and anger. Physical and sexual violence, as well as the constant underlying threat of violence, are pervasive among prison systems, especially in the United States. Inmates display emotions ranging from anger to fear to despair. Conditions are often overcrowded and borderline dilapidated. One must wonder what Dostoevsky would think about modern society if he were to visit a correctional institution.

Moreover, we have to consider that the public would not be accepting of violence in the community to the extent that it exists in the prison environment. Indeed this has been proven by the rigid approaches to crime control in recent decades. By passing legislation that stipulates long prison sentences, even for minor offenses, society has sought to send a message that crime and violence will not be tolerated. Why are we unwilling to send a similar message to those serving time? Why do we accept continued crime and violence behind bars, even at the expense of the larger community?

The recommendations provided in this final chapter represent a mere start to approaching the issue. Although the United States' "crime epidemic" (and similar epidemics of other nations) has been ameliorated in the past few decades, it has been replaced with nothing short of a prison epidemic. By addressing the needs of our prison population, we can show that we are abandoning our "lock them up and throw away the key" mentality that has guided our criminal justice policies, and that we are moving toward a more civilized approach.

References

Adams, K. 1992. Adjusting to prison life. *Crime and Justice*, 16, 275–359.

Aday, R.H. 1994. Golden years behind bars: Special programs and facilities for older inmates. *Federal Probation*, 58(2), 47–54.

Aday, R.H. 2003. *Aging prisoners: Crisis in American Corrections*. Westport: Praeger.

Alarid, L.F. 2000. Sexual perspectives of incarcerated bisexual and gay men: The county jail protective custody experience. *The Prison Journal*, 80(1), 80–95.

Albrecht, H.J. 1997. Sentencing and punishment in Germany, in *Sentencing Reform in Overcrowded Times,* edited by M.H. Tonry and K. Hatlestad. New York: Oxford University Press, pp. 181–187.

Allard, T.J., Wortley, R.K. and Stewart, A.L. 2008. The effect of CCTV on prison misbehavior. *The Prison Journal*, 88(3), 404–422.

Allen, B. and Bosta, D. 1981. *Games Criminals Play*. Susanville, CA: Rae John Publishers.

Anderson, E. 2000. *The Code of the Street: Decency, Violence and the Moral Code of the Inner City.* New York: W.W. Norton.

Andrews, D.A. and Bonta, J. 2003. *The Psychology of Criminal Conduct*. Cincinnati: Anderson.

Anirudha, K. 2005. *Judicial inspectorate of prisons review of decision made on 18 Nov 2003.* http://www.pmg.org.za/docs/2005/050624strydom.htm [accessed: December 12, 2011]

Arditti, J.A. 2005. Families and incarceration: An ecological approach. *Families in Society: The Journal of Contemporary Social Services*, 86(2), 251–260.

Atlas, R. 1983a. Crime site selection for assaults in four Florida prisons. *The Prison Journal,* 63(1), 59–72.

Atlas, R. 1983b. Weapons used in prison assault: A profile of four Florida prisons. *Aggressive Behavior*, 9(2), 125–131.

Austin, J., Fabelo, T., Gunter, A. and McGinnis, K. 2006. S*exual Violence in the Texas Prison System*. Washington, D.C.: National Institute of Justice.

Austin, J. and Irwin, J. 2012. *It's About Time: America's Imprisonment Binge.* 4th Edition. Belmont, CA: Wadsworth.

Bales, W.D. and Mears, D.P. 2008. Inmate social ties and the transition to society: Does visitation reduce recidivism? *Journal of Research in Crime and Delinquency*, 45(3), 287–321.

Banbury, S. 2004. Coercive sexual behavior in British prisons as reported by adult ex-prisoners. *The Howard Journal,* 43(2), 113–130.

Banking on bondage: Private prisons and mass incarceration. 2011. Online: American Civil Liberties Union. Available at: www.aclu.org/prisoners-rights/banking-bondage-private-prisons-and-mass-incarceration [accessed: March 10, 2012].

Baskin, D., Sommers, I. and Steadman, H. 1991. Assessing the Impact of Psychiatric

Impairment on Prison Violence. *Journal of Criminal Justice*, 19(3), 271–280.

Beccaria, C. 1764. *Of Crimes and Punishments*. New York, Oxford University Press.

Beck, A. 2011. PREA Data Collection Activities, 2011. Bureau of Justice Statistics. Washington, D.C.: U.S. Department of Justice. NCJ 234183

Beck, A.J. and Harrison, P.M. 2007. Sexual victimization in state and federal prisons reported by inmates, 2007, Bureau of Justice Statistics. Washington, D.C.: U.S. Department of Justice. NCJ 219414.

Beck, A.J., Harrison, P.M. and Adams, D.B. 2007. Sexual violence reported by correctional authorities, 2006. Bureau of Justice Statistics. Washington, D.C.: U.S. Department of Justice. NCJ 218914.

Beck, A.J., Harrison, P.M., Berzofsky, M., Caspar, R. and Krebs, C. 2010. Sexual victimization in prisons and jails reported by inmates, 2008–2009. Bureau of Justice Statistics. Washington, D.C.: U.S. Department of Justice. NCJ 231169.

Becker, H. 1963. *Outsiders*. New York: Free Press.

Bench, L.L. and Allen, T.D. 2003. Investigating the stigma of prison classification: An experimental design. *The Prison Journal*, 83(4), 367–382.

Bennett, J. 2006. The good, the bad and the ugly: The media in prison films. *The Howard Journal of Criminal Justice* 45(2), 97–115.

Berk, R.A., Kriegler, B. and Baek, J. 2006. Forecasting dangerous inmate misconduct: An application of ensemble statistical practices. *Journal of Quantitative Criminology*, 22(2), 131–145.

Biere, D.M. 2011. Is tougher better? The impact of physical prison conditions on inmate violence. *International Journal of Offender Therapy and Comparative Criminology*, 20(5), 1–18.

Biermans, N. and D'Hoop, M. 2001. *Development of Belgian prisons into a restorative justice perspective.* Positioning Restorative Justice Conference. (Leuven, Belgium. September 16–19 2001).

Bilchik, S. 2007. Mentoring: A promising intervention for children of prisoners. *Research in Action,* 10, 3–28. Alexandria, VA: Mentor.

Blackburn, A.G., Mullings, J.L. and Marquart, J.W. 2008. Sexual assault in prison and beyond: Toward an understanding of lifetime sexual assault among incarcerated women. *The Prison Journal*, 88(3), 351–377.

Blevins, K.R., Listwan, S.J., Cullen, F.T. and Johnson, C.L. 2010. A general strain theory of prison violence and misconduct: An integrated model of inmate behavior. *Journal of Contemporary Criminal Justice*, 26(2), 148–166.

Blumberg, M. and Laster, J.D. 2009. The impact of HIV/AIDS on corrections, in *Prisons and Jails: A Reader*, edited by R. Tewksbury and D. Dabney. New York: McGraw Hill, 291–304.

Blumstein, A. and Beck, A.J. 1999. Population growth in U.S. prisons, 1980–1996, in *Prisons: Crime and Justice – A Review of the Research, Volume 26,* edited by M. Tonry and J. Petersilia. Chicago: University of Chicago Press, 17–61.

Bobbitt, M., Campbell, R. and Tate, G.L. 2011. Safe return: Working toward preventing domestic violence when men return from prison. *Federal Sentencing Reporter*, 24(1), 57–61.

Bohannon, J. 2009. The theory? Diet causes violence. The Lab? Prison. *Science*, 325(5948), 1614–1616.

Boone, M. and Moerings, M. 2007. Growing prison rates, in *Dutch Prisons*, edited by M. Boone and M. Moerings. The Hague: BJU Legal Publishers, 341–448.

Bordieu, P. 2001. *Masculine Domination*. Palo Alto, CA: Stanford University Press.

Bottoms, A.E. 1999. Interpersonal violence and social order in prison. *Crime and Justice*, 26: 205–281.

Bowker, L.H. 1980a. *Prison Victimization*. New York, NY: Elsevier.

Bowker, L.H. 1980b. Victimizers and victims in American correctional institutions, in *The Pains of Imprisonment,* edited by R. Johnson and H. Toch. Beverly Hills: Sage, 63–76.

Bowker, L.H. 1983. An essay on prison violence. *The Prison Journal*, 63, 24–31.

Boxer, P., Middlemass, K. and Delorenzo, T. 2009. Exposure to violent crime during incarceration: Effects on psychological adjustment following release. *Criminal Justice and Behavior,* 36(8), 793–807.

Boxer, P., Schappell, A., Middlemass, K. and Mercado, I. 2011. Cognitive and emotional covariates of violence exposure among former prisoners: Links to antisocial behavior and emotional distress and implications for theory. *Aggressive Behavior*, 37, 465–475.

Bradley, R.G. and Davino, K.M. 2002. Women's perceptions of the prison environment: When prison is "the safest place I've ever been". *Psychology of Women Quarterly*, 26, 351–359.

Braithwaite, J. 1989. *Crime, Shame and Social Reintegration*. Cambridge: Cambridge University Press.

Braman, D. 2005. Families and incarceration, in *The Effects of Imprisonment*, edited by A. Liebling and S. Maruna. Cullompton, Devon: Willan Publishing, 117–135.

Briggs, C.S., Sundt, J.L. and Castellano, T.C. 2003. Effect of supermaximum security prisons on aggregate levels of institutional violence. *Criminology,* 41(4), 1341–1376.

Brookman, F., Copes, H. and Hochstetler, A. 2011. Street codes as formula stories: How inmates recount violence. *Journal of Contemporary Ethnography*, 40(4), 397–424.

Brown v. Plata. 2011. No. 09-1233

Brown v. Board of Education. 1954. 347 U.S. 483

Brown, A.K. 2005. *Jurors reject Texas prison rape lawsuit*. Stop Prisoner Rape. Available at: www.spr.igc.org/en/news/2005/1018.htm [accessed: November 12, 2011].

Brown, D. 1998. Penality and imprisonment in Australia, in *Comparing Prison Systems: Toward a Comparative and International Penology*, edited by R.P. Weiss and N. South. Amsterdam: Gordon and Breach, 367–400.

Browne, A., Cambier, A. and Agha, S. 2011. Prisons within Prisons: The use of segregation in the United States. *Federal Sentencing Reporter*, 24(1), 46–49.

Bulman, P. 2009. Using technology to make prisons and jails safer. *NIJ Journal* [online], March, 38–41. Available at: www.nij.gov/journals/262/corrections-technology.htm [accessed: January 4, 2012].

Byrne, J. and Hummer, D. 2007. In search of the "Tossed Salad Man" (and others involved in prison violence): New strategies for predicting and controlling violence in prison. *Aggression and Violent Behavior*, 12(5), 531–541.

Byrne, J. and Hummer, D. 2008. Examining the impact of institutional culture on prison violence and disorder: An evidence-based review, in *The Culture of Prison Violence* edited by. J.M. Byrne, D. Hummer and F. Taxman. Boston: Pearson, 40–66

Byrne, J.M., Hummer, D. and Stowell, J. 2008. Prison violence, prison culture, and offender change: New directions for research, theory, policy and practice, in *The Culture of Prison Violence*, edited by J.M. Byrne, D. Hummer and F. Taxman. Boston: Pearson, 202–219

Byrne, J.M., Hummer, D. and Taxman, F.S. 2008. The National Institute of Corrections' institutional culture change initiative: A multisite evaluation, in *The Culture of Prison Violence,* edited by J.M. Byrne, D. Hummer and F. Taxman. Boston: Pearson, 137–163.

Calhoun, A. and Coleman, H. 2002. Female inmates' perspectives on sexual abuse by correctional personnel: An exploratory study. *Women and Criminal Justice 13*,101–124.

Camp, C.G. 2003. *Corrections Yearbook, 2002*. Middletown, CT: Criminal Justice Institute.

Camp, C.G. and Camp, G.M. 2001. *Corrections Yearbook, 2000*. Middletown, CT: Criminal Justice Institute.

Camp, S.D. and Gaes, G.G. 2005. Criminogenic effects of the prison environment on inmate behavior: Some experimental evidence. *Crime and Delinquency*, 51, 425–442.

Camp, S.D., Saylor, W.G. and Wright, K.N. 2000. Racial diversity of correctional workers and inmates: Organization commitment, teamwork and worker efficacy in prisons. Federal Bureau of Prisons. Available at: www.bop.gov/news/research_projects/published_reports/equity_diversity/oreprcamp_jq2.pdf - 2008-07-17 [accessed December 12, 2011]

Campbell, C. 1997. Migrancy, masculine identities and AIDS: The psychosocial context of HIV transmission on the South African gold mines. *Social Science Medicine*, 45(2), 273–281.

Carlson, P.M. and Garrett, J.S. 2008. *Prison and Jail Administration: Practice and Theory*. Sudbury, MA: Jones and Bartlett.

Carrabine, E. 2005. Prison riots, social order and the problem of legitimacy. *British Journal of Criminology*, 45, 896–913.

Casey, K.A. and Wiatrowski, M.D. 1996. Women offenders and "three strikes and you're out", in *Three Strikes and You're Out: Vengeance as Public Policy*, edited by D. Schichor and D.K. Sechrest. Thousand Oaks, CA: Sage, 222–243.

Casey-Acevedo, K. and Bakken, T. 2001. The effects of visitation on women in prison. *International Journal of Comparative and Applied Criminal Justice*, 25, 48–69.

Cavadino, M. and Dignan, J. 2006. *Penal Systems: A Comparative Approach*. Thousand Oaks: Sage.

Chaneles, S. 1987. Growing old behind bars. *Psychology Today*, 21(1), 47–51.

Chapman, B., Mirrlees-Black, C. and Brown, C. 2002. *Improving Public Attitudes to the Criminal Justice System: The Impact of Information*. London: HMSO.

Cheeseman, K. 2003. Importing aggression: An examination and application of subculture theories to prison violence. *The Southwest Journal of Criminal Justice*, 1(1), 24–38.

Cheeseman, K., Mullings, J. and Marquart, J. 2001. Inmate Perceptions of Staff Across Various Custody Levels of Security. *Corrections Management Quarterly*, 5, 41–48.

Chesney-Lind, M. 2002. Imprisoning women: The unintended victims of mass imprisonment, in *Invisible punishment: The collateral consequences of mass imprisonment*, edited by M. Mauer and M. Chesney-Lind. New York: The New Press, 136–149. China to classify prisons by security levels. Embassy of the People's Republic of China in the United States of America. Available at: www.china-embassy.org/eng/gyza/t200492.htm [accessed: April 14, 2012].

Cid, J. 2009. Is imprisonment criminogenic? A comparative study of recidivism rates between prison and suspended prison sanctions. *European Journal of Criminology*, 6(6), 459–480.

Clemmer, D. 1940. *The prison community*. Boston: Christopher Publishing House.

Codd, H. 2008. *In the shadow of prison: Families, imprisonment and criminal justice*. Cullompton, Devon: Willan Publishing.

Cohen, L. and Felson, M. 1979. Social change and crime rate trends: A routine activity approach. *American Sociological Review*, 44(4), 588–608.

Collica, K. 2002. Levels of knowledge and risk perceptions about female inmates in New York State: Can prison-based HIV programs set the stage for behavior change? *The Prison Journal*, 82(1), 101–124.

Comfort, M. 2003. In the tube at San Quentin: The "secondary prisonization" of women visiting inmates. *Journal of Contemporary Ethnography*, 32(1), 77–107.

Comparative imagination. 2011. *Probation Journal*, 58(4), 311–316.

Continuing Gang Threat. 2011. Federal Bureau of Investigation. Available at www.fbi.gov/news/stories/2011/october/gangs_102011 [accessed November 2, 2012].

Cooke, D.J., Wozniak, E. and Johnstone, L. 2008. Casting light on prison violence in Scotland: Evaluating the impact of situational risk factors. *Criminal Justice and Behavior,* 35(8), 1065–1078.

Cooley, D. 1993. Criminal victimization in male federal prisons. *Canadian Journal of Criminology*, 35: 479–495.

Corlew, K.R. 2006. Congress attempts to shine a light on a dark problem: An in-depth look at the Prison Rape Elimination Act of 2003. *American Journal of Criminal Law*, 33(2), 157–190.

Cornish, D.B. and Clarke, R.V. 2003. Opportunities, precipitators and criminal decisions: A reply to Wortley's critique of situational crime prevention, in *Theory for Practice in Situational Crime Prevention. Crime Prevention Studies*, Vol. 16, edited by M.A. Smith and D.B. Cornish. Monsey, NY: Willan, 41–96.

Cotton, D.J. and Groth, A.N. 1982. Inmate rape: Prevention and intervention. *Journal of Prison and Jail Health,* 2(1), 47–57.

Crawley, E. and Crawley, P. 2008. Culture, performance and disorder: The communicative quality of prison violence, in *The Culture of Prison Violence*, edited by J.M. Byrne, D. Hummer, and F.S. Taxman. Boston: Pearson, 123–136.

Crawley, E. and Sparks, R. 2006. Is there life after imprisonment? How elderly men talk about imprisonment and release. *Criminology ad Criminal Justice*, 6(1), 63–82.

Crewe, B. 2005. Prisoner society in the era of hard drugs. *Punishment and Society*, 7(4), 457–481.

Crouch, B. and Marquart, J.W. 1980. On becoming a prison guard, in *The Keepers Prison guards and contemporary corrections*, edited by B. Crouch. Springfield, IL: Charles C. Thomas, 63–106.

Culp, R.F. 2005. Frequency and characteristics of prison escapes in the United States: An analysis of national data. *The Prison Journal*, 85(3), 270–291.

Cunningham, M.D. and Sorenson, J.R. 2007. Predictive factors for violent misconduct in close custody. *The Prison Journal,* 87(2), 241–253

Dabney, D.A. and Vaughn, M.S. 2000. Incompetent jail and prison doctors. *The Prison Journal*, 80(2), 151–183.

Dalton, V. 1999. Prison homicide in Australia: 1980–1998. Trends and issues in crime and criminal justice, 103. Canberra: Australian Institute of Criminology.

Day, A. 1998. Cruel and unusual punishment of female inmates: The need for redress under 42 U.S.C. *Santa Clara Law Review,* 38(2), 555–587.

DeLisi, M. 2003. Criminal careers behind bars. *Behavioral Sciences and the Law*, 21(5), 653–669.

de Maillard, J. and Roche, S. 2004. Crime and justice in France: Time trends, policies and political debate. *European Journal of Criminology*, 1(1), 111–151.

Devilly, D.J., Sorbello, L., Eccleston, L. and Ward, T. 2005. Prison-based peer education schemes. *Aggression and Violent Behavior*, 10, 219–240.

Dhami, M.K., Mantle, G. and Fox, D. 2009. Restorative justice in prisons. *Contemporary Justice Review*, 12(4), 433–448.

Diamond, B., Morris, R.G., Barnes, J.C. 2012. Individual and group IQ predict inmate violence. *Intelligence*, 40(2), 115–122.

Dickens, C. 1842. Philadelphia, and its solitary prison. *American Notes*.

Dunkle, F. 1996. *Empirische Forschung Im Strafvollzug*. Bonn: Forum Verlag Godesberg.

DiIulio, J.J. 1987. *Governing Prisons*. New York: Free Press.

Dobash, R.P., Dobash, R.E. and Gutteridge, S. 1986. *The imprisonment of women*. New York: Basil Blackwell.

Donaldson, S. 2001. A million jockers, punks and queens: Sex among American male prisoners and its implications for concepts of sexual orientation in. In *Prison masculinities*, edited by D. Sabo, T.A. Kupers and W. London. Philadelphia: Temple University Press, 118–126.

Donaldson, S. 2003. Hooking up: Protective pairing for punks, in *Violence in War and Peace: An Anthology*, edited by N. Scheper-Hughes and P. Bourgois. Williston, VT: Blackwell Publishing, 348–353.

Dorozynski, A. 2000. Doctor's book shames French prisons. *British Medical Journal*, 320(7233), 465. Available at: www.nbml.nlm.nih.gov/pmc/articles/pmc1127522 [accessed: January 14, 2012].

Drury, A.J. and DeLisi, M. 2011. Gangkill: An exploratory empirical assessment of gang membership, homicide offending and prison misconduct. *Crime & Delinquency*, 57(1), 130–146.

Dumond, R.W. 1992. The sexual assault of male inmates in incarcerated settings. *International Journal of the Sociology of Law*, 20(2), 135–157.

Dumond, R.W. 2000. Inmate sexual assault: The plague that persists. *The Prison Journal*, 80(4), 407–414.

Durkheim, E. 1893 *The division of labor in society*. New York: The Free Press.

Durkheim, E. 1897. *Suicide*

Easteal, P. 2001. Women in Australian prisons: The cycle of abuse and dysfunctional environments. *The Prison Journal*, 81(1), 87–112.

Eddy, J.M. and Reid, J.B. 2002. The antisocial behavior of the adolescent children of incarcerated parents: A developmental perspective. From Prison to Home Conference, Washington, D.C., January 30–31, 2002.

Edgar, K. 2005. Bullying, victimization and safer prisons. *Probation Journal*, 52, 390–400.

Edgar, K. 2008. Cultural roots of violence in England's prisons: An exploration of inter-prisoner conflict, in *The Culture of Prison Violence*, edited by J.M. Byrne, D. Hummer and F. Taxman. Boston: Pearson, 180–197.

Edgar, K., O'Donnell, I. and Martin, C. 2003. *Prison violence: The dynamics of conflict, fear and power.* Cullompton Devon, UK: Willan Publishing.

Edgar, K. and Martin, C. 2000. *Conflicts and violence in prison.* Research findings from the ESRC Violence Research Programme. Available at: www.rhbnc. ac.uk/sociopolitical-science/vrp/findings/rfedgar.pdf [accessed October 12, 2011].

Eigenberg, H.M. 1989. Male rape: An empirical examination of correctional officers' attitudes toward male rape in prison. *The Prison Journal*, 68(2), 39–56.

Eigenberg, H.M. 2000. Correctional officers and their perceptions of homosexuality, rape and prostitution in male prison. *The Prison Journal*, 80(4), 415–433.

Einat, T. 2009. Inmate harassment and rape: An exploratory study of seven maximum and medium security male prisons in Israel. *International Journal of Offender Therapy and Comparative Criminology*, 53(6), 648–664.

Ellenbogen, P. 2009. Beyond the border: A comparative look at prison rape in the United States and Canada. *Columbia Journal of Law and Social Problems*, 42, 335–372.

Ellis, D.P. and Austin, P. 1971. Masturbation and aggressive behavior in a correctional center for women. *The Journal of Criminal Law, Criminology and Police Science* 62(3), 388–395.

Essuon, A.D., Simmons, D.S., Stephens, T.T., Richter, D., Lindley, L.L. and Braithwaite, R.L. 2009. Transient populations: Linking HIV, migrant workers, and South African male inmates. *Journal of Health Care for the Poor and Underserved*, 20 (2A), 40–52.

Estelle v. Gamble, 429 U.S. 97 (1976)

Fagan, T.J. 2003. Mental health in corrections: A model for service delivery, in *Correctional Mental Health Handbook* edited by T.J. Fagan and R.K. Ax. Thousand Oaks, CA: Sage Publications, 3–19.

Fairweather, C. 2002. Safeguarding the public, promoting correctional excellence. *Corrections Today*, 64(1), 38–41.

Farmer v. Brennan 1994. 511 U.S. 825

Faulkner, P.L. and Faulkner, W.R. 2006. Effects of organizational change on inmate status and the inmate code of conduct, in *Behind Bars: Readings on Prison Culture,* edited by R. Tewksbury. Upper Saddle River, NJ: Pearson, 75–86.

Federal Ministry of the Interior and Federal Ministry of Justice. 2006. Second periodical report on crime and crime control in Germany. Berlin.

Feest, J. 1998. *Reducing the prison population: Lessons from the West German experience.* London: NACRO.

Feest, J. 1999. Imprisonment and prisoners work: Normalization or less eligibility?*Punishment and Society*, 1(1): 99–107.

Feest, J. and Weber, H.M. 1998. Germany: Ups and downs in the resort to imprisonment-strategic or unplanned outcomes? In *Comparing Prison*

Systems: Toward a Comparative and International Penology, edited by R. Weiss and N. South, 233–261.

Felson, M. 2009. *Crime and everyday life*. Thousand Oaks, CA Sage.

Fernandez, M. 2011. In bid to cut costs at some Texas prisons, lunch will not be served on weekends. *The New York Times*. October 20. Available at: http://www.nytimes.com/2011/10/21/us/texas-reduces-weekend-meals-for-prisoners.html [accessed March 29, 2012].

Finn, P. 2000. Addressing correctional officer stress: Programs and Strategies. National Institute of Justice. Washington, D.C., U.S. Department of Justice.

Finn, P. 2009. Correctional officer stress: A cause for concern and additional help, in *Prisons and Jails: A Reader*, edited by R. Tewksbury and D. Dabney). New York: McGraw Hill, 207–220.

Fitzgerald, M. and Sim, J. 1982. *British Prisons*. London: Basil Blackwell.

Fleisher, M.S. and Decker, S.H. 2007. Gangs behind bars: Prevalence, conduct and response, in *Prisons and Jails: A Reader*, edited by R. Tewksbury and D. Dabney. New York: McGraw Hill, 159–174.

Flynn, E. 2000. Elders as perpetrators, in *Elders, Crime and the Criminal Justice System: Myth, Perceptions and Reality in the 21st century*, edited by M. Rothman and B. Dunlop. New York: Springer, 43–83.

Foster, T. 1975. Make-believe families: A response of women and girls to the deprivation of imprisonment. *International Journal of Criminology and Penology*, 3, 71–78.

Foucault, M. 1977. *Discipline and Punish: The Birth of the Prison*. New York: Vintage.

Freiberg, A. 2001. Three strikes and you're out – it's not cricket: Colonization and resistance in Australian sentencing, in *Sentencing and Sanctions in Western Countries*, edited by M.H. Tonry and R.S. Frase. New York: Oxford University Press, 30–61.

Gaes, G.G. and Goldberg, A.L. 2004. Prison rape: A Critical review of the literature. Washington, D.C.: U.S. Department of Justice, National Institute of Justice. NCJ 213365.

Gaes, G.G. and McGuire, W.J. 1985. Prison violence: The contribution of crowding versus other determinants of prison assault rates. *Journal of Research in Crime and Delinquency*, 22, 41–65.

Gaes, G., Wallace, S., Gilman, E., Klein-Saffran, J. and Suppa, S. 2002. The influence of prison gang affiliation on violence and other prison misconduct. *The Prison Journal*, 82(3), 359–385.

Gallo, E. 1995. The penal system in France: From correctionalism to managerialism, in *Western European Penal Systems: A Critical Anatomy*, edited by V. Ruggiero, M. Ryan, and J. Sim. London: Sage, 71–92.

Gear, S. 2007. Behind the bars of masculinity: Male rape and homophobia in and about South African men's prisons. *Sexualities*, 10(2), 209–227.

Geraci, P.M. 2003. A Japanese prison visit: Yokosuka. *Journal of Correctional Education*, 54(3), 87.

Giallombardo, R. 1966. *Society of women: A study of a woman's prison*. New York: Wiley.

Gibbons, J. 2011. Confronting confinement: A report on the commission on safety and abuse in America's prisons. *Federal Sentencing Reporter – General Federal Materials*, 24 (1), 36–41.

Gibbons, J. and Katzenbach, N.B. 2006. *Confronting confinement: A report of the commission on safety and abuse in America's prisons*. New York: Vera Institute of Justice.

Gilligan, J. 2002 How to increase the rate of violence – and why, in *Exploring Corrections: A Book of Readings*, edited by T. Gray. Boston: Allyn and Bacon, 200–214.

Glaze, L.E. 2010. Correctional populations in the United States, 2009, U.S. Department of Justice. Bureau of Justice Statistics. NCJ 231681.

Glaze, L.E. 2011. Correctional populations in the United States, 2010. U.S. Department of Justice. Washington, D.C.: Bureau of Justice Statistics. NCJ 236319

Glaze, L.E. and Bonczar, T.P. 2011. Probation and parole in the United States, 2010. Bureau of Justice Statistics. Washington, D.C.: U.S. Department of Justice. NCJ 236019

Goffman, E. 1961. *Asylums: Essays on the social situation of mental patients and other inmates*. Anchor books.

Goode, E. 2002. Drug arrests at the Millennium." *Social Science and Public Policy*. July/August, 41–45.

Gordon, A.F. 2009. The United States military prison: The normalcy of exceptional brutality, in *The Violence of Incarceration*, edited by P. Scraton and J. McCulloch. New York: Routledge, 164–186.

Goyer, K. 2002. Prison health in public health: HIV/AIDS and the case for prison reform. *South African Crime Quarterly*, Nov.2. Available at: www.iss.co.za/pubs/crimeQ/No.2/ 5Goyer.html [accessed: July 1, 2011].

Goyer, K. 2003. HIV/AIDS in prisons: Problems policies and potential. Pretoria, Institute for Security Studies. Monograph 79. Available at: www.iss.co.za/pubs/monograph/no79/content.html [accessed: July 22. 2011].

Goyer, K.C. and Gow, J. 2001. Transmission of HIV in South African prisons: Risk variables. *Society in transition,* 32(1), 128–132.

Graczyk, M. 2012. Leader of "Texas 7" prison-break gang put to death. *Houston Chronicle* (February 29). Available at: http://www.chron.com/news/article/Leader-of-Texas-7-prison-break-gang-put-to-death-3370673.php [accessed March 22, 2012].

Graffam, J., Shinkfield, A.J. and Hardcastle, L. 2008. The perceived employability of ex-prisoners and offenders. *International Journal of Offender Therapy and Comparative Criminology, 52,* 673–685.

Grann, D. 2004. The brand: How the Aryan brotherhood became the most murderous prison gang in America. *The New Yorker* (February 16), 157–171.

Green, B.L., Miranda, J., Daroowalla, A. and Siddique, J. 2005. Trauma exposure, mental health functioning, and program needs of women in jail. *Crime and Delinquency*, 51(1), 133–151.

Greenberger, M. 2007. You ain't seen nothing yet: The inevitable post-Hamden conflict between the Supreme Court and the political branches. *Maryland Law Review*, 66, 805–807.

Griffin, M. 2007. Prison gang policy and recidivism: Short-term management benefits, long-term consequences. *Criminology and Public Policy*, 6, 223–230.

Grounds, A. and Jamieson, R. 2003. No sense of an ending: Researching the experience of imprisonment and release among Republican ex-prisoners. *Theoretical Criminology*, 7(3), 347–362.

Guerino, P., Harrison, P.M. and Sabol, W.J. 2011. Prisoners in 2010. Bureau of Justice Statistics. Washington, D.C.: U.S. Department of Justice. NCJ 234183.

Guidoni, O.V. 2003. The ambivalence of restorative justice: Some reflections on an Italian prison project. *Contemporary Justice Review*, 6(1), 55–68.

Hagemann, O. 2008. Conditions of imprisonment – Victimization and conflict in European prisons. *Journal of Ethnicity in Criminal Justice*, 6(4), 281–302.

Hairston, C.F. 2001. The forgotten parent: Understanding the forces that influence incarcerated fathers' relationships with their children, in *Children with parents in prison: Child welfare policy, program, and practice issues,* edited by C. Seymour and C.F. Harrison. New Brunswick, NJ: Transaction Publishers, 149–171.

Halberstadt, R.L. and La Vigne, N.G. 2011. Evaluating the use of radio frequency identification device (RFID) technology to prevent and investigate sexual assaults in a correctional setting. *The Prison Journal*, 91(2), 227–249.

Hamai, K. and Ellis, T. 2008. Japanese criminal justice: Was reintegrative shaming a chimera? *Punishment and Society*, 10(1), 25–46.

Hamm, M.S. 2008. Prisoner radicalization: Assessing the threat in U.S. correctional institutions. *National Institute of Justice Journal*, 261. Available at: http://www.nij.gov/journals/261/prisoner-radicalization.htm [accessed: March 9, 2012].

Hammett, T., Harmon, P. and Maruschak, L.L. 1999. *1996–1997 update: HIV/ AIDS, STDs, and TB in correctional facilities.* Washington, D.C.: National Institute of Justice.

Haney, C. 2003. Mental health issues in long-term solitary confinement. *Crime and Delinquency*, 49, 124–156.

Harer, M.D. and Langan, N.P. 2001. Gender differences in predictors of prison violence: Assessing the predictive validity of a risk classification system. *Crime & Delinquency,* 47(4), 513–536.

Harlow, C.W. 2003. *Education and correctional populations* Bureau of Justice Statistics. Washington, D.C.: U.S. Department of Justice, Bureau of Justice Statistics. NCJ 195670.

Harne, J. and Scott, F. 2009. NIJ tests new technologies. *Corrections Today*, 71(4), 88–89.

Harrison, L.D. 2001. The revolving prison door for drug-involved offenders: Challenges and opportunities. *Crime and Delinquency*, 47(3), 462–484.

Harrison, B. and Schehr, R. 2004. Offenders and post-release jobs: Variables influencing success and failure. *Journal of Offender Rehabilitation, 39(3)*, 35–68.

Hart, S.V. 2003. Making prisons safer through technology. *Corrections Today*, 65(2).

Hartman, K.E. 2008. Supermax prisons in the consciousness of prisoners. *The Prison Journal*, 88(1), 169–176.

Hassine, V. (2010). *Life Without Parole: Living and Dying in prison Today.* 5th Edition. New York: Oxford University Press.

Hefferman, E. 1972. *Making it in prison: The square the cool, and the life.* New York: Wiley.

Heiner, R. 2005. The growth of incarceration in The Netherlands. *Federal Sentencing Reporter,* 17(3), 227–230.

Henderson, M. 2001. Employment and crime: What is the problem and what can be done about it from the inmate's perspective. *Corrections Management Quarterly, 5,* 36–42.

Hensley, C. 2000. Attitudes toward sexuality in a male and female prison: An exploratory study. *The Prison Journal*, 80(4), 434–441.

Hensley, C., Koscheski, M. and Tewksbury, R. 2003. The impact of institutional factors on officially reported sexual assaults in prison. *Sexuality and Culture,* 7(4), 16–26.

Hensley, C., Struckman-Johnson, C. and Eigenberg, H.M. 2000. Introduction: The history of prison sex research. *The Prison Journal,* 80(4), 360–367.

Hensley, C. and Tewksbury, R. 2005. Wardens' perceptions of inmate fear of sexual assault: A research note. *The Prison Journal*, 85(2), 198–203.

Hensley, C., Tewksbury, R. and Castle, T. 2003. Characteristics of prison sexual assault in male Oklahoma correctional facilities. *Journal of Interpersonal Violence,* 18(6), 595–606.

Hensley, C., Wright, J., Tewksbury, R. and Castle, T. 2003. The evolving nature of prison argot and sexual hierarchies. *The Prison Journal,* 83(3), 289–300.

Hirschi, T. 1969. *Causes of Delinquency.* Los Angeles: University of California Press. HM Inspectorate of Prisons. 2005. Old and quiet – No problem, *Thematic review of older prisoners.* London: HM Inspectorate of Prisons.

HM Prison Service. 2006. Violence reduction strategy, Prison Service Order 2750. Available at: http://pso.hmprisonservice.gov/uk/PSO_2750_violence_ reduction.doc [accessed: August 1, 2011].

Hochstetler, A. and DeLisi, M. 2005. Importation, deprivation and varieties of serving time: An integrated-lifestyle-exposure model of prison offending. *Journal of Criminal Justice,* 33(3), 257–266.

Hollandsworth, S. 2001. Maximum insecurity. *Texas Monthly*, 29(3), 23–25.

Holmes, S.T. and Holmes, R.M. 2009. *Sex crimes: Patterns and behaviors.* Los Angeles: Sage.

How much does it cost to incarcerate an inmate? (2009) Legislative Analyst's Office. Available at: http://www.lao.ca.gov/laoapp/laomenus/sections/crim_justice/6_cj_inmatecost.aspx [accessed: September 12, 2011].

Hughes, T., Wilson, D. and Beck, A. 2001. Trends in state parole, 1990–2000. Bureau of Justice Statistics. Washington, D.C.: U.S. Department of Justice. NCJ 184735.

Hunt G., Riegel, S., Morales, T. and Waldorf, D. 1993. Changes in prison culture: Prison gangs and the case of the "Pepsi generation". *Social Problems,* 40(3), 398–409.

Immigration detention. ACLU website. Available at: www.aclu.org/immigrants-rights/detention. [accessed: March 18, 2012].

I'm still in that box: 23 years in solitary confinement. ACLU website. Available at: www.aclu.org/prisoners-rights/im-still-box-23-years-solitary-confinement [Accessed: April 13, 2012].

In the shadows: Sexual violence in U.S. detention facilities. 2006. Los Angeles: Stop Prisoner Rape.

Ireland, J.L. 1997. Bullying amongst prisoners: A study of gender differences, provictim attitudes and empathy. MSC dissertation. Manchester, U.K.: The Manchester Metropolitan University.

Ireland, J.L. and Archer, J. 1996. Descriptive analysis of bullying in male and female adult prisons. *Journal of Community Applied Social Psychology*, 6, 35–47.

Ireland, C.A. and Ireland, J.L. 2006. Descriptive analysis of the nature and extent of bullying behavior in a maximum-security prison. In *Behind Bars: Readings on Prison Culture,* edited by R. Tewksbury. Upper Saddle River, NJ: Pearson, 87–96.

Irwin, J. and Cressey, D.R. 1962. Thieves, convicts and the inmate culture. *Social Problems*, 10, 142–155.

Irwin, J. and Owen B. 2005. Harm and the contemporary prison, in *The effects of imprisonment,* edited by A. Liebling and S. Maruna. Cummompton, Devon: Willan Publishing. 94–117.

Jacobs, J.B. 2007. Finding alternatives to the carceral state. *Social Research*, 74(2), 695–699.

James, D.J. and Glaze, L.E. 2006. Mental health problems of prison and jail inmates. Bureau of Justice Statistics. Washington, D.C.: U.S. Department of Justice.

Jamieson, R. and Grounds, A. 2005. Release and adjustment: Perspectives from studies of wrongly convicted and politically motivated prisoners, in *The Effects of Imprisonment*, edited by A. Libling and S. Maruna). Cullompton, Devon, Willan Publishing, 33–65.

Jemelka, R., Rahman, S. and Trupin, E. 1993. Prison mental health: An overview, in *Mental Illness in America's Prisons*, edited by H.J. Steadman and J.J. Cocoza. Seattle: National Coalition for the Mentally Ill in the Criminal Justice System, 9–23.

Jiang, S. and Fischer-Giorlando, M. 2002. Inmate misconduct: A test of the deprivation, importation and situational models. *The Prison Journal*, 82, 335–358.

Johansen, V.A., Wahl, A.K., Eiertsen, D.E. and Weisaeth, L. 2007. Prevalence and predictors of post-traumatic stress disorder (PTSD) in physically injured victims of non-domestic violence: A longitudinal study. *Social Psychiatry and Psychiatric Epidemiology*, 42, 583–593.

Johnson, R. 2006. Prowling the yard: The public culture of the prison, in *The Dilemmas of Corrections: Multidisciplinary Perspectives*, edited by K.C. Haas and G.P. Alpert. Long Grove, IL: Waveland Press, 171–210.

Johnson v. California. 2005. 321 F.3d791.

Johnston, D. 1995. Effects of parental incarceration, in *Children of incarcerated parents*, edited by K. Gabel and D. Johnston. New York: Lexington Books, 59–68.

Joint Working Group, OUT LGBT Wellbeing and Durban Lesbian and Gay Community and Health Centre. 2005. Fact sheet: Experiences of human rights violations in Kwa-Zulu Natal, 2004/2005.

Jones, T.R. and Pratt, T.C. 2008. The prevalence of sexual violence in prison: The state of the knowledge base and implications for evidence-based correctional policy making. *International Journal of Offender Therapy and Comparative Criminology*, 52(3), 280–295.

Kappeler, V.E. and Potter, G.W. 2005. *The Mythology of Crime and Criminal Justice*. 4th Edition. Long Grove, IL: Waveland Press.

Kelly, V.G., Merrill, G.S., Shumway, M., Alvidrez, J. and Boccellari, A. 2010. Outreach engagement and practical assistance: Essential aspects of PTSD care for urban victims of violence crime. *Trauma, Violence and Abuse*, 11(3), 144–156.

Kersting, K. 2003. New hope for sex offender treatment. *Monitor on Psychology*, 34(7), 52.

Keys, D.P. 2002. Instrumental Sexual Scripting: An examination of gender-role fluidity in the correctional institution. *Journal of Contemporary Criminal Justice, 18(3),* 258–278.

King, R.D. 1998. Prisons. In *Handbook of crime and punishment*, edited by M. Tonry. New York: Oxford University Press, 589–625.

Knowles, G. J. 1999. Male prison rape: A search for causation and prevention. *The Howard Journal*, 38(3), 267–282.

Knox, G.W. 2005. The problem of gangs and security threat groups in American prisons today: Recent research findings from the 2004 Prison Gang Survey. Peotone, IL: National Gang Crime Research Center.

Krienert, J. and Fleisher, M. 2005. "It ain't happening here": Working to understand prison rape. *The Criminologist*, 30(6), 1–5

Kruttschnitt, C. and Dirkzwager, A. 2011. Are there still contrasts in tolerance? Imprisonment in the Netherlands and England 20 years later. *Punishment & Society*, 13(3), 283–306.

Kupers, T. 1999. *Prison madness: The mental health crisis behind bars and what we must do about it.* San Francisco: Jossey-Bass.

Lambert, E.G., Hogan, N.L., Barton, S. and Stevenson, M.T. 2007. An evaluation of CHANGE, a prison cognitive treatment program. *Journal of Articles in Support of the Null Hypothesis*, 5(1), 1–17.

Landreth, G.L. and Lobaugh, A.F. 1998. Filial therapy with incarcerated fathers: Effects on parental acceptance of child, parental stress, and child adjustment. *Journal of Counseling and Development*, 76, 157–165.

Lankenau, S.E. 2001. Smoke 'em if you got 'em: Cigarette black markets in U.S prisons and jails. *The Prison Journal*, 81(2), 142–161.

Latimer, J., Dowden, C. and Muise, D. 2005. The effectiveness of restorative justice processes: A meta-analysis. *The Prison Journal*, 85(2), 127–144.

Lawrence, S. and Travis, J. 2004. *The new landscape of imprisonment: Mapping America's prison expansion.* Washington, D.C.: The Urban Institute.

Lemert, E.M. 1951. *Social pathology.* New York: McGraw-Hill.

Levan, K. 2007. A routine activities approach to sexual assault behind bars. Paper presented at The American Society of Criminology Annual Meeting, Atlanta, GA, November, 2007.

Levan, K. 2011. Gangs and violence, in *Key Issues in Crime and Punishment: Corrections,* edited by W. J. Chambliss. Thousand Oaks, CA: Sage, 105–118.

Levan-Miller, K. 2008. 'That don't happen here': Techniques of neutralization and inmate perceptions of sexual assault. Unpublished paper. Paper presented at The American Society of Criminology Annual Meeting, St. Louis, MO, November, 2008.

Levan-Miller, K. 2010. The Darkest Figure of Crime: Perceptions of Reasons for Male Inmates to not Report Sexual Assault. *Justice Quarterly*, 27(5), 1–21.

Levan, K., Polzer, K. and Downing, S. 2011. Media and prison sexual assault: How we got to the "Don't drop the soap" culture. *International Journal of Criminology and Sociological Theory*, 4(2), 674–682.

Levenson, J. 2001. Inside Information: Prisons and the Media. *Criminal Justice Matters* 43, 14–15.

Liebling, A. 2008. Why prison staff culture matters, in *The Culture of Prison Violence* edited by J.M. Byrne, D. Hummer, and F.S. Taxman. Boston: Pearson, 105–122.

Light, S.C. 1991. Assaults on prison officers: Interactional themes. *Justice Quarterly*, 8, 243–261.

Lippert, R. 2009. Signs of the surveillant and assemblage: Privacy, regulation, urban CCTV, and governmentality. *Social and Legal Studies*, 18(4), 505–522.

Lipsey, M., Landenberger, N. and Wilson, S. 2007. Effects of cognitive-behavioral programs for criminal offenders. Campbell Systematic Reviews, 6. Available at: www.campbellcollaboration.org/lib/download143 [accessed: January 12, 2012]. List of detainee deaths in ICE custody. ICE website. Available at: www.ice.gov/doclib/foia/reports/detainee**deaths**2003-present.pdf [accessed: March 18, 2012].

Lockwood, D. 1980. Prison sexual violence. New York: Elsevier.

Lockwood, D. 1982. The Condition of sexual harassment to stress and coping in confinement. In *Coping with Imprisonment*, edited by N. Parisi. Beverly Hills: Sage, 45–64.

Lommel, J. 2004. Turning around turnover. *Corrections Today*, 66(5), 54–57.

Love, N. 2011. Report: NH female inmates not treated same as men. *Boston Globe*. Available at: www.boston.com/news/local/new-hampshire/articles/2011/10/17/report_being_released_on_nh_prisons [accessed on: October 17].

Lovell, D., Cloyes, K., Allen D. and Rhodes, L. 2000. Who lives in supermax custody? A Washington state study. *Federal Probation*, 64, 33–38.

Lovell, D. and Jemelka, R. 1998. Coping with mental illness in prison. *Family and Community Health*, 21(3), 54–66.

Lurigio, A.J. and Snowden, J. 2008. Prison culture and the treatment and control of mentally ill offenders, in *The Culture of Prison Violence*, edited by J.M. Byrne, D. Hummer and F. Taxman. Boston: Pearson, 164–179.

Lynch, M. 2011. Mass incarceration, legal change, and locale: Understanding and remediating American penal overindulgence. *Criminology and Public Policy*, 10(3), 673–698

McCorkle, R.C. 1992. Personal precautions to violence in prison. *Criminal Justice and Behavior*, 19, 160–173.

McCorkle, R.C. 1993. Fear of victimization and symptoms of psychopathology among prison inmates. *Journal of Offender Rehabilitation*, 19(1/2), 27–41.

McCorkle, R., Miethe, T. and Drass, K. 1995. The roots of prison violence: A test of the deprivation, management, and "not so total" institutional models. *Crime and Delinquency*, 41(3), 317–331.

McCulloch, J. and George, A. 2009. Naked power: Strip searching in women's prisons, in *The Violence of Incarceration*, edited by P. Scraton and J. McCulloch. New York: Routledge, 107–123.

McCulloch, J. and Scraton, P. 2009. The violence of incarceration: An introduction, in *The Violence of Incarceration*, edited by P. Scraton and J. McCulloch. New York: Routledge, 1–18.

McGurk, B., Forde, R. and Barnes, A. 2000. Sexual victimization among 15–17 year old offenders in prison. RDS Occasional Paper 65. London: Home Office.

MacKenzie, D.L. 2006. *What works in corrections: Reducing the criminal activities of offenders and delinquents.* New York: Cambridge University Press.

MacKenzie, D.L., Robinson, J.W. and Campbell, C.S. 1989. Long-term incarceration of female offenders. *Criminal Justice and Behavior*, 16, 223–238.

McKinney, D. 2012. Ex-inmate on controversial prison: "Tamms never leaves my head". *The Sun Times,* March 27, Available at: naperville.suntimes.com/news/10862646-417/ex-inmate-on-controversial-prison-tamms-never-leaves-my-head.html [accessed: April 13, 2012].

McShane, M.D. 2008. *Prisons in America.* New York: LFB Scholarly Publishing.

Maitland, A. and Sluder, R. 1996. Victimization in prisons: A study of factors related to the general well-being of youthful inmates. *Federal Probation*, 60(2), 24–31.

Maitland, A. and Sluder, R. 1998. Victimization and youthful prison inmates: An empirical analysis. *The Prison Journal*, 78(1), 55–73.

Making Corrections Safer With Technology. 2008. *Corrections Today*, 70(1), 62–63.

Man, C.D. and Cronan, J.P. 2001. Forecasting sexual abuse in prison: The prison subculture of masculinity as a backdrop for "deliberate indifference". *The Journal of Criminal Law and Criminology*, 92(1), 127–185.

Mariner, J. 2001. No escape: Male rape in U.S. prisons. Human Rights Watch. Available at: www.hrw.org/reports/2001/prison/report.html [accessed August 15, 2011].

Marquez, J. and Thompson, D. 2006. Prison "peacekeeper" wielded influence. Associated Press, January 22. Available at: nctimes.com/articles/2006/01/23/news/state/12206193342.txt [accessed: February 2, 2012].

Martinson, R. 1974. "What works?" Questions and answers about prison reform. *Public Interest*, 35, 22–54.

Maruschak, L.M. 2009. HIV in prisons, 2007–2008. Bureau of Justice Statistics. Washington, D.C.: U.S. Department of Justice. NCJ 228307

Mason, C. 2012. *Too good to be true: Private prisons in America*. Washington, D.C.: The Sentencing Project.

Mason, P. 2003. The screen machine: Cinematic representations of prisons. In P. Mason (Ed.) *Criminal visions: Media representations of crime and justice*. Cullompton: Willan Publishing, 278–297.

Mason, T.R. 1982. The epitome of failure: Jack Abbott. *Crime and Delinquency*, 28(1), 557–566.

Mathieson, T. 2001. Television, public space and prison population: A commentary on Mauer and Simon. *Punishment and Society* 3(1), 35–42.

Mauer, M. 2001. The causes and consequences of prison growth in the United States. *Punishment and Society* 3(1), 9–20.

Mauer, M. 2006a. Comparative international rates of incarceration: An examination of causes and trends, in *The Dilemmas of Corrections: Multidisciplinary Perspectives*, edited by K.C. Haas and G.P. Alpert. Long Grove, IL: Waveland Press, 79–89.

Mauer M. 2006b. Racial disparity and the criminal justice system: An assessment of causes and responses, in *The Dilemmas of Corrections: Multidisciplinary Perspectives*, edited by K.C. Haas and G.P. Alpert. Long Grove, IL: Waveland Press, 98–119.

Mauer, M. 2011. Addressing the political environment shaping mass incarceration. *Criminology & Public Policy*, 10(3), 699–705.

Mears, D.P. 2004. Mental health needs and services in the criminal justice system. *Houston Journal of Health Law and Policy*, 4, 255–284.

Mears, D.P. 2008. Accountability, efficiency, and effectiveness in corrections:

Shining a light on the black box of prison systems. *Criminology and Public Policy*, 7(1), 143–152.

Meiners, E. 2007. Life after Oz: Ignorance, mass media, and making public enemies. *The Review of Education, Pedagogy and Cultural Studies* 29: 23–63.

Merton, R.K. 1942. The normative structure of science, in *The Sociology of Science: Theoretical and Empirical Investigations,* edited by R.K. Merton. Chicago, IL: University of Chicago Press, 267–278.

Miller, W. 1958. Lower class culture as a generating milieu of gang delinquency. *Journal of Social Issues*, 14, 5–19.

Mingdi, W. Human rights protection in China's prisons. China's Human Rights. Available at: www.humanrights-china.org/zt/situation/20040200410159052. htm [accessed: April 20, 2012].

Money, J. and Bohmer, C. 1980. Prison sexology: Personal accounts of masturbation, homosexuality and rape. *The Journal of Sex Research,* 16(3), 258–266.

Montgomery, R. and Crews, G. 1998. *A History of Correctional Violence: An Examination of Reported Causes of Riots and Disturbances.* Lantham, MD: American Correctional Association.

Moore, S. 2009. Hundreds hurt in California prison riot. *The New York Times*, August 9. Available at: www.nytimes.com/2009/08/10/us/10prison.html [accessed: March 12, 2012].

Morash, M., Jeong, S.J. and Zang, N.L. 2010. An exploratory study of the characteristics of men known to commit prisoner-on-prisoner sexual violence. *The Prison Journal*, 90(2), 161–178.

Moster, A.N. and Jeglic, E.L. 2009. Prison warden attitudes toward prison rape and sexual assault: Findings since the Prison Rape Elimination Act (PREA). *The Prison Journal*, 89(1), 65–78.

Mumola, C.J. 2005. Suicide and homicide state prisons and local jails. Bureau of Justice Statistics. Washington, D.C.: U.S. Department of Justice. NCJ 210036.

Mumola, C.J. and Karberg, J.C. 2006. Drug use and dependence, state and federal prisoners, 2004. Bureau of Justice Statistics. Washington, D.C.: U.S. Department of Justice. NCJ 213530.

Muntingh, L. 2009. Reducing prison violence: Implications from the literature for South Africa. CSPRI Research Report No. 17. Civil Society Prison Reform Initiative. Community Law Centre. Western Cape, South Africa: University of Western Cape.

National Institute of Corrections. 2003. Institutional Culture Initiative, Program Meeting, Washington, D.C.

Nelken, D. 2011. Review symposium on Nicola Lacey, The Prisoners' Dilemma: Political economy and punishment in contemporary democracies: Explaining differences in European rates: A comment on Lacey's The Prisoners' Dilemma. *Punishment and Society*, 13(1), 104–114.

Nerenberg, R. 2002. Spotlight: Condoms in correctional settings. The Body: The Complete HIV/AIDS Resource. Available at: www.thebody.com/content/art13017.html [accessed: July 1, 2011].

Neser, J.J. and Pretorius, M. 1993. AIDS in prisons. *Acta Criminologica,* 6(1), 1.

Newburn, T. 2007. 'Tough on crime': Penal policy in England and Wales, in *Crime, punishment and politics in comparative perspective. Crime and justice: A review of research, Vol. 36,* edited by M. Tonry. Chicago: University of Chicago Press, 425–470.

Newell, T. 2002. Restorative practice in prisons: Circles and conferencing in the custodial setting. Paper presented at the Third International Conference on Conferencing, Circles, and Other Restorative Practices. Minneapolis, MN.

Noonan, M.E. and Carson, E.A. 2011. *Prison and jail deaths in custody, 2000–2009. Statistical tables.* Bureau of Justice Statistics. Washington, D.C.: US Department of Justice. NCJ 236219

Notorious Texas Seven. 2008. America's Most Wanted. Available at: http://www.amw.com/features/feature_story_detail.cfm?id=2754&mid=0 [accessed March 20, 2012].

O'Donnell, I. 2004. Prison rape in context. *British Journal of Criminology 44,* 241–255.

O'Donnell, I. and Edgar, K. 1996. *The extent and dynamics of victimization in prisons.* London: HMSO.

O'Donnell, I. and Edgar, K. 1998. Routine victimization in prisons. *The Howard Journal,* 37(3), 266–279.

Olweus, D. 1994. Annotation: Bullying at school: Basic facts and effect s of a school based intervention program. *Journal of Child Psychology and Psychiatry,* 35, 1171–1190.

Onishi, N. 2008. Japan: Prisons to adapt to older inmates. *The New York Times.* January 5, 2.

Oppel, R.A. 2011. Private prisons found to offer little in savings. The New York Times. Available at: www.nytimes.com/2011/05/19/us/19prisons.html?pagewanted=all [accessed: March 17, 2012].

Owen, B., McCampbell, S.W. and Wells, J.W. 2007. Staff perspectives: Sexual violence in adult prisons and jails. Washington, D.C.: National Institute of Corrections/The Moss Group.

Owen, B. and Wells, J.W. 2006. Staff perspectives: Sexual violence in adult prisons and jails. Washington, D.C.: National Institute of Corrections/The Moss Group.

Page, J. 2002. Violence and incarceration: A personal observation, in *Correctional Perspectives: Views from Academics, Practitioners and Prisoners,* edited by L. Alarid and P. Cromwell. Los Angeles, CA: Roxbury Publishers, 138–141.

Page, S. 2009. Poll: Most opposed closing Gitmo. *USA Today.* June 2, 1A.

Palestinian prisoners in Israeli's prisons – Facts and figures. 2008. Adaleh – The Legal Center for Minority Rights in Israel. Available at: www.adaleh.org/newsletter/eng.apr08.pdf [accessed: April 12, 2012].

Parfitt, T. 2010. Crime and unjust punishment in Russia. *The Lancet*, 376: 1815–1816.

Pease, K. 1991. Talk at the Annual General Meeting of the British Society of Criminology. Unpublished paper.

Pease, K. 1992. Punitiveness and prison populations: An international comparison. *Justice of the Peace*, 156, 405–408.

Pease, K. 1994. Cross-national imprisonment rates: Limitations of method and possible conclusions. *British Journal of Criminology*, 34, 116–130.

Perez, D.M., Gover, A.R., Tennyson, K.M. and Santos, S.D. 2010. Individual and institutional characteristics related to inmate victimization. *International Journal of Offender Therapy and Comparative Criminology*, 54(3), 378–394.

Perkinson, R. 1994. Shackled justice: Florence federal penitentiary and the new politics of punishment. *Social Justice*, 21(3), 117–123.

Petersilia, J. 2003. *When prisoners come home: Parole and prisoner reentry.* New York: Oxford University Press.

Petersilia, J. 2008. Prisoner re-entry: Public safety and reintegration challenges, in *Prisons and Jails: A Reader,* edited by R. Tewksbury and D. Dabney. Boston: McGraw Hill, 545–560.

Phillips, C. 2012. "It ain't nothing like America with the Bloods and the Crips": Gang narratives inside two English prisons. *Punishment and Society*, 14(1), 51–68.

Pizarro, J.M., Stenius, V.M.K. and Pratt, T.C. 2006. Supermax prisons: Myths, realities and the politics of punishment in American society. *Criminal Justice Policy Review*, 17(1), 6–21.

Pogrebin, M.R. and Dodge, M. 2001. Women's accounts of their prison experiences: A retrospective view of their subjective realties. *Journal of Criminal Justice (21)*, 531–541.

Porporino, F.J., Doherty, P.D., and Sawatsky, T. 1987. Characteristics of homicide victims and victimization in prisons: A Canadian historical perspective. *International Journal of Offender Therapy and Comparative Criminology*, 31(2), 125–153.

Pratt, T.C. 2009. *Addicted to Incarceration.* Thousand Oaks, CA: Sage.

Pratt, J. and Clark, M. 2005. Penal populism in New Zealand. *Punishment and Society*, 7(3), 303–322.

Prison Rape Elimination Act of 2003. Public Law 108–79. Sept. 4, 2003.

Quinn, J.F. 2003 *Corrections: A Concise Introduction.* Second Edition. Long Grove, IL: Waveland Press.

Reiman, J. and Leighton, P. 2010. *The Rich Get Richer and the Poor Get Prison: Ideology, Class and Criminal Justice*. 9th Edition. Boston: Allyn & Bacon.

Reynolds, M. 2008. The War on Drugs, prison building and globalization: Catalysts for the global incarceration of women. NWSA Journal, 20(2), 72–95.

Rhodes, L.A. 2004. *Total confinement: Madness and reason in the maximum security prison.* Berkeley and Los Angeles: University of California Press.

Richie, B.E. 2002. The social impact of mass incarceration on women, in *Invisible punishment: The collateral consequences of mass imprisonment*, edited by M. Mauer and M. Chesney-Lind. New York: The New Press, 136–149.

Richters, J., Butler, T., Schneider, K., Yap, L., Kirkwood, K., Grant, L., Richards, A., Smith, A. and Donovan, B. 2012. Consensual sex between men and sexual violence in Australian prisons. *Archives of Sexual Behavior*, 41(2), 517–524.

Riveland, C. 1999. Prison management trends, 1975–2025, in *Prisons,* edited by M.H. Tonry and J. Petersilia. Chicago: University of Chicago Press, 163–203.

Rivera, B.D., Cowles, E.L. and Dorman, L.G. 2003. An exploratory study of institutional change: Personal control and environmental satisfaction in a gang-free prison. *The Prison Journal*, 83(2), 149–170.

Rose, C.D., Reschenberg, K, and Richards, S.C. 2010. The inviting convicts to college program. *Journal of Offender Rehabilitation, 49(4),* 293–308.

Ross, J.I. 2008. *Special problems in corrections.* Upper Saddle River, NJ: Pearson Education.

Ross, J.I. 2011. Moving beyond Soering: U.S. prison conditions as an argument against extradition to the United States. *International Criminal Justice Review*, 21(2), 156–168.

Ross, J.I. and Richards, S.C. 2003. *Convict Criminology.* Belmont, CA: Wadsworth. Rothstein, M. 1999. *Employment Law.* St. Paul: West Group.

Rotter, M. and Steinbacher, M. 2001. The clinical impact of doing time – Mental illness and incarceration, in *Forensic Mental Health: Working With Offenders With Mental Illness* edited by G. Landsberg and A. Smiley. New Jersey: CVI, 16-1–16-6.

Ruddell, R., Decker, S.H. and Egley, A. 2006. Gang interventions in jails: A national analysis. *Criminal Justice Review*, 31(1), 33–46.

Sabbath, M.J. and Cowles, E.L. 1992. Problems associated with long term incarceration. *Forum on Corrections Research*, 4(2), 9–11.

Sabol, W.J. and West, H.C. 2010. Prisoners in 2009. Bureau of Justice Statistics. Washington, D.C.: U.S. Department of Justice. NCJ 231675.

Sattar, G. 2004 Prisoner-on-prisoner homicide in England and Wales between 1990 and 2001. Research and Statistics, Home Office. Available at: www. webarchive.nationalarchives.gov.uk [accessed July 23, 23.2011].

Scarpa, A. 2001. Community violence exposure in a young adult sample: Lifetime prevalence and socioemotional effects. *Journal of Interpersonal Violence*, 16, 36–53.

Scarpa, A. 2003. Community violence exposure in young adults. *Trauma, Violence and Abuse*, 4, 210–227.

Scarpa, A., Fikretoglu, D., Bowser, F., Hurley, J.D., Pappert, C.A., Romero, N. and Van Vorhees, E. 2002. Community violence exposure in university students: A replication and extension. *Journal of Interpersonal Violence*, 17: 253–272.

Schaufeli, W.B. and Peeters, M.C.W. 2000. Job stress and burnout among correctional officers: A literature review. *International Journal of Stress Management*, 7(1), 19–48.

Schoenfeld, H. 2010. Mass incarceration and the paradox of prison conditions litigation. *Law and Society Review*, 44, 731–768.

Schumaker, R., Anderson, D. and Anderson, S. 1990. Vocational and academic indicators of parole success. *Journal of Correctional Education, 41*, 8–13.

Scott, G. 2001. Broken windows behind bars: Eradicating prison gangs through ecological hardening and symbol cleansing. *Corrections Management Quarterly*, 5(1), 23–36.

Scraton, P. 2009. Protests and 'riots' in the violent institution, in *The Violence of Incarceration*, edited by P. Scraton and J. McCulloch. New York: Routledge, 60–85.

Sechrest, D.K. 1991. The effects of density on jail assaults. *Journal of Criminal Justice, 25*, 61–73.

Seiter, R.P. 2011. *Corrections: An Introduction.* 3rd Edition. Saddle River, J: Pearson.

Serving Time: Prisoner diet and Exercise. 2006. London: HM Prison Service.

Shelden, R.G. 2010. *Our punitive society: Race, class, gender and punishment in America.* Long Grove, IL: Waveland Press.

Sigurdson, C. 2000. The mad, the bad, and the abandoned: The mentally ill in prisons and jails. *Corrections Today*, (December), 70–78.

Sisco, M.M. and Becker, J.V. 2007. Beyond predicting the risk of sexual victimization in prison – Considering inmate options and reporting avenues for addressing an inherent problem. *Criminology and Public Policy*, 6(3), 573–584.

Skinner, B.F. 1938. *The Behavior of Organisms: An Experimental Analysis.* New York: Appleton-Century.

Slotbloom, A., Bijleveld, C., Day, S. and Van Giezen, A. 2008. *Detained women in the Netherlands: On importation and deprivation factors in detention-damage.* Amsterdam: Vrije Universiteit.

Slotbloom, A., Kruttschnitt, C., Bijleveld, C. and Menting, B. 2011. Psychological well-being of incarcerated women in the Netherlands: Importation or deprivation? *Punishment & Society, 13*(2), 176–197.

Snacken, S. 2005. Forms of violence and regimes in prison: Report of research in Belgian prisons, in *The effects of imprisonment,* edited by A. Liebling and S. Maruna. Cullumpton, Devon: Willan Publishing, 306–309.

Snacken, S. 2010. Resisting punitiveness in Europe? *Theoretical Criminology*, 14, 273–292.

Sorenson, J. and Cunningham, M.D. 2010. Conviction offenses and prison violence: A comparative study of murderers and other offenders. *Crime & Delinquency*, 56(1), 103–125.

Sorenson, J. and Davis, J. 2011. Violent criminals locked up: Examining the effect of incarceration on behavioral continuity. *Journal of Criminal Justice*, 39, 151–158. Sourcebook of criminal justice statistics online. 2004. Bureau of Justice Statistics. Available at: www.albany.edu/sourcebook/pdf/t5482004.pdf [accessed: February 2, 2012].

Spelman, W. 2000. The limited importance of prison expansion, in *The Crime Drop in America*, edited by A. Blumstein and J. Wallman. Cambridge, UK: Cambridge University Press, 97–129.

Spencer, R. 2009. Gitmo inmates will spread Jihad in U.S. prisons. *Human Events*, 65(20), 17.

Spivak, A.L. and Sharp, S.F. 2008. Inmate recidivism as a measure of private prison performance. *Crime and Delinquency*, 54(3), 482–508.

Statistics of offences against prison discipline and punishments in England and Wales. Various years. H.M. Stationery Office.

Steiner, B. and Woolredge, J. 2009. Individual and environmental effects on assaults and nonviolent rule breaking by women in prison. *Journal of Research in Crime and Delinquency*, 46(4), 437–467.

Steinke, P. 1991. Using situational factors to predict types of prison violence. *Journal of Offender Rehabilitation,* 17, 119–132.

Stern, V. 2002. Prisoners as citizens: A comparative view. *Probation Journal*, 49(2), 130–193.

Stevens, J. 2010. America's secret ice castles. *The Nation*. January 4. Available at: http://www.thenation.com/article/americas-secret-ice-castles [accessed: March, 18, 2012].

Stinchcomb, J.B. 2010. *Corrections: Foundations for the Future*. 2nd Edition. New York: Routledge.

Stowell, J.I, and Byrne, J.M. 2008. Does what happens in prison stay in prison? Examining the reciprocal relationship between community and prison culture, in *The Culture of Prison Violence,* edited by J.M. Byrne, D. Hummer, and F. Taxman. Boston: Pearson, 27–39.

Struckman-Johnson, C. and Struckman-Johnson, D. 2000. Sexual coercion rates in seven Midwestern prison facilities for men. *The Prison Journal,* 80(4), 379–380.

Struckman-Johnson, C. and Struckman-Johnson, D. 2002. Sexual coercion reported by women in three Midwestern prisons. *The Journal of Sex Research* 39(3), 217–227.

Struckman-Johnson, C., Struckman-Johnson, D., Rucker, L., Bumby, K. and Donaldson, S. 1996. Sexual coercion reported by men and women in prison. *The Journal of Sex Research* 33(1), 67–76.

Sturges, J.E. 2002. Visitation at county jails: Potential policy implications. *Criminal Justice Policy Review*, 13, 32–45.

Sundt, J., Castellano, T.C. and Briggs, C.S. 2008. The sociopolitical context of prison violence and its control: A case study of supermax and its effect in Illinois. *The Prison Journal*, 88(1), 94–122.

Sutherland, E. 1939. *Principles of Criminology*. Philadelphia: J.B. Lippincott.

Sykes, G.M. 1958. *The society of captives*. Princeton: University Press.

Sykes, G.M. and Matza, D. 1957. Techniques of neutralization: A theory of delinquency. *American Sociological Review,* 22.

Sykes, G.M. and Messinger, S. 1960. The inmate social system, in *Theoretical Studies in Social Organization of the Prison*. New York: Social Science Research Council. 5–19.

Tak, P.J. 2001 Sentencing and punishment in the Netherlands, in *Sentencing and Sanctions in Western Countries*, edited by M. Tonry and R.S. Frase. New York: Oxford University Press, 151–187.

Tartaro, C. 2002. The impact of density on jail violence. *Journal of Criminal Justice*, 30, 499–510.

Taxman, F.S., Perdoni, M.L. and Harrison, L.D. 2007. Drug treatment services for adult offenders: The state of the state. *Journal of Substance Abuse Treatment*, 32(3), 239–254.

Terry, C.M. 2000. Beyond punishment: Perpetuating difference from the prison experience. *Humanity and Society*, 24(2), 108–135.

Terry, C.M. 2003. Managing prisoners as problem populations and the evolving nature of imprisonment: A convict perspective. *Critical Criminology*, 12, 43–66.

Tewksbury, R. 2010. Prisons in the last ten years. *Victims & Offenders*, 5(3), 240–252.

Tewksbury, R. and DeMichele, M. 2005. Going to prison: A prison visitation program. *The Prison Journal*, 85, 292–310.

Thomas, G., Farrell, M.P. and Barnes, G.M. 1996. The effects of single mother families and nonresident fathers on delinquency and substance abuse in black and white adolescents." *Journal of Marriage and Family*, 58, 884–894.

Thomas, P.A. and Moerings, M. (Eds). 1994. *AIDS in prison*. Hants, England: Darmouth Publishing Company Ltd.

Time, V.A. 2012. Lessons learned about low crime rates in Japan: Field notes from interviews with Japanese police officers, in *Crime Prevention*,edited by D.A. Mackey and K. Levan. Burlington, MA: Jones and Bartlett.

Toch, H. 1977. Living in prison: *The ecology of survival*. New York: Free Press.

Toch, H. 1985. Social climate and prison violence, in *Prison Violence in America*, edited by M. Braswell, R. Montgomery and L. Lombardo Cincinnati: Anderson Publishing.

Toch, H. and Adams, K. 1987. The prison as dumping ground: Mainlining disturbed offenders. *Journal of Psychiatry and Law*, 15, 539–553.

Toch, H. and Kupers, T.A. 2007. Violence in prisons revisited. *Journal of Offender Rehabilitation*, 45(3/4), 1–28.

Tonry, M. 2001. Punishment policies and patterns in Western countries, in *Sentencing and Sanctions in Western Countries*, edited by M.H. Tonry and R.S. Frase. New York: Oxford University Press, 3–28

Trammel, R. 2009. Relational violence in women's prison: How women describe interpersonal violence and gender. *Women & Criminal Justice*, 19, 267–285.

Trammel, R. 2011. Symbolic violence and prison wives: Gender roles and protective pairing in men's prisons. *The Prison Journal*, 91(3), 305–324.

Trammell, R. 2012. *Enforcing the Convict Code: Violence and Prison Culture*. Boulder, CO: Lynne Rienner.

Travis, J. 2008. Families and children. In *Prisons and Jails: A Reader*, edited by R. Tewksbury and D. Dabney. Boston: McGraw Hill, 335–350.

Travis, J., McBride, E.C. and Solomon, A.L. 2003. Families left behind: The hidden costs of incarceration and reentry. The Urban Institute. Available at www.urban.org/publications/310882.html [accessed: August 15, 2011].

Trulson, C.R., Marquart, J.W., Hemmens, J.W. and Carroll, L. 2008. Racial desegregation in prisons. *The Prison Journal*, 88(2), 270–299.

Trulson, C.R., Marquart, J. and Kawucha, S. 2006. Gang suppression and institutional control. *Corrections Today*, 68, 26–30.

Truman, J.L. 2011. Criminal victimization, 2010. Bureau of Justice Statistics. Washington, D.C.: U.S. Department of Justice. NCJ 235508.

Turner, A. 2007. Automated video surveillance – Improving CCTV to detect and prevent incidents. *Corrections Today,* 69(3), 44–51.

Turner, M.G., Sundt, J.L., Applegate, B.K. and Cullen, F.T. 1995. "Three strikes and you're out" legislation: A national assessment. *Federal Probation,* 59(3), 16–35.

Ullrich, S. and Coid, J. 2011. Protective factors for violence among released prisoners – effects over time and interactions with static risk. *Journal of Consulting and Clinical Psychology*, 79(3), 381–390.

Umbreit, M.S., Coates, R.B. and Vos, R. 2006. The impact of victim-offender mediation: Two decades of research, in *The Dilemmas of Corrections: Multidisciplinary Perspectives*, edited by K.C. Haas and G.P. Alpert. Long Grove, IL: Waveland Press, 476–491.

Underwood, M.A., Galen, B.R. and Paquette, J.A. 2001. Top ten challenges for understanding gender and aggression in children: Why can't we all just get along? *Social Development,* 10(2), 248–266.

U.S. Immigration and Customs Enforcement Salaries and Expenses, Fiscal Year, 2012 Congressional Budget Justification. Department of Homeland Security. Available at www.dhs.gov/xlibrary/assets/dhs-congessonal-budget-justification-fy2012.pdf [accessed: March 18, 2012].

Useem, B. and Piehl, A.M. 2006. Prison buildup and disorder. *Punishment and Society*, 8(1), 87–115.

Useem, B. and Reisig, M.D. 1999. Collective action in prisons: Protests, disturbances and riots. *Criminology*, 37(4), 735–760.

Van Gemmert, A.A. 2002. *Report women in detention*. Ministrie van Justice: Den Haag, DJI.

Vannoy, S.D. and Hoyt, W.T. 2004. Evaluation of an anger therapy intervention for incarcerated male adults. *Journal of Offender Rehabilitation,* 39(2), 39–57.

Van Voorhis, P. and Presser, L. 2001. *Classification of women offenders: A national assessment of current practices*. Washington, D.C.: U.S. Department of Justice, Bureau of Justice Statistics.

Van Zyl Smit, D. 2004. Swimming against the tide, in *Justice Gained? Crime and crime control in South Africa's transition,* edited by B. Dixon and E. van der Spuy Cullompton: Willan Publishing, 227–258.

Vassuer, V. 2000. *Chief Doctor at La Santé Prison.* Paris: Le Cherche midi.

Vaughn, M.S. and del Carmen, R. 1995. Civil liability against prison officials for inmate-on-inmate assault: Where are we, and where have we been? *The Prison Journal*, 75(1) 69–89.

Vito, G.F. and Wilson, D.G. 1985. Forgotten people: Elderly inmates. *Federal Probation*, 49(1), 18–23.

Wacquant, L. 2001. Deadly symbiosis: When ghetto and prison meet and mesh. *Punishment and Society* 3 (1), 95–134.

Wakefield, S. and Wildeman, C. 2011. Mass imprisonment and racial disparities in childhood behavioral problems. *Criminology & Public Policy,* 10(3), 793–817.

Waller, J.M. 2003. Testimony before the subcommittee on terrorism, technology and homeland security. United States Senate Committee on the Judiciary. Available at: http://www.judiciary.senate.gov/hearings/testimony. cfm?id=4f1e0899533f7680e7 8d03281ff19bc6&wit_id=4f1e0899533f7680 e78d03281ff19bc6-2-1 [accessed on March 19, 2012].

Walmsley, R. 2009. World prison population list, 8th Edition. National Institute of Corrections. Washington, D.C.: U.S. Department of Justice.

Walrath, E. 2001. Evaluation of a prisoner run alternatives to violence project – The impact of inmate-to-prisoner intervention. *Journal of Interpersonal Violence,* 16(7), 697–711.

Walshe, S. 2012. Righting the record on prison rape. *The Guardian.* March 1. Available at: www.guardian.co.uk/commentisfree/cifamerica/2012/mar/01/ shareholder-crusade-prison-rape[accessed: March 9, 2012].

Wang, E., Owens, R., Long, S., Diamond, P. and Smith, J. 2000. The effectiveness of rehabilitation with persistently violent male prisoners. *International Journal of Offender Therapy and Comparative Criminology*, 44, 505–514.

Ward, S.A. 2009. Career and technical education in United States prisons: What have we learned? *The Journal of Correctional Education*, 60(3), 191–200.

Ward, D.A. and Kassebaum, G. G. 1965. *Women's Prison: Sex and Social Structure.* Aldine Press: Chicago.

Weigend, T. 1997. German reduces use of prison sentences, in *Sentencing Reform in Overcrowded Times: A Comparative Reader*, edited by M. Tonry and K. Hatlestad. New York: Oxford University Press, 177–181.

Welch, M. 2009. Guantanamo Bay as a Foucauldian phenomenon: An analysis of penal discourse, technologies, and resistance. *The Prison Journal*, 89(1), 3–20.

Wheeler, S. 1961. Socialization in correctional communities. *American Sociological Review*, 26, 697–712.

Whitworth, A. 2010. Detecting contraband: Current and emerging technologies and limitations. *Corrections Today*, 105–107. October.

Wilczak, G.L. and Markstrom, C.A. 1999. The effects of parent education on parental focus of control and satisfaction of incarcerated fathers. *International Journal of Offender Therapy and Comparative Criminology*, 43(1), 90–102.

Wilkinson, R. and Pickett, K. 2009. *The spirit level: Why more equal societies always do better.* London: Allen Lane.

Wilkinson, R.A. and Unwin, T. 1999. Intolerance in prison: A recipe for disaster. *Corrections Today*, 61–98.

Wobeser, W.L., Datema, J., Bechard, B. and Ford, P. 2002. Causes of death among people in custody in Ontario, 1990–1999. *Canadian Medical Association Journal,* 167(10), 1109–1113.

Wolfgang, M. and Ferracuti, F. 1967. *The Subculture of Violence: Towards an Integrated Theory in Criminology.* London: Tavistock Publications.

Wolff, N., Blitz, C.L., Shi, J., Siegel, J. and Bachman, R. 2007. Physical violence inside prisons: Rates of victimization. *Criminal Justice and Behavior*, 34(5), 588–599.

Wolff, N. and Shi, J. 2009. Contextualization of physical and sexual assault in male prisons: Incidents and their aftermath. *Journal of Correctional Health Care*, 15(1), 58–77.

Wolff, N., Shi, J. and Bachman, R. 2008. Measuring victimization inside prisons: Questioning the questions. *Journal of Interpersonal Violence*, 23(10), 1342–1362.

Wolff, N., Shi, J. and Blitz, C. 2008. Racial and ethnic disparities in types and sources of victimization inside prison. *The Prison Journal*, 88(4), 451–472.

Women in prison: Sexual misconduct by correctional staff. 1999. Washington, D.C.: United States General Accounting Office. Available at: www.gao.gov/archive/1999/gg99104.pdf [accessed: January 4, 2012].

Wood, J. 2006. Gang activity in English prisons: The prisoners' perspective. *Psychology, Crime and Law*, 12(6), 605–617.

Wooden, W.S. and Parker, J. 1982. *Men behind bars: Sexual exploitation in prison.* New York: Plenum.

Woolredge, J.D. 1998. Inmate lifestyles and opportunities for victimization. *Journal of Research in Crime and Delinquency*, 35, 480–502.

Woolredge, J.D. and Steiner, B. 2009. Comparing methods for examining relationships between prison crowding and inmate violence. *Justice Quarterly*, 26(4), 795–826.

Wozniak, E. 1989. Inverness segregation unit, in *Current issues in Scottish prisons: Systems of accountability and regimes for difficult prisoners, edited by E. Wozniak.* Edinburgh, UK: HMSO. 86–113.

Wright, K. and Goodstein, L. 1989. Correctional Environments. In *The American prison system: Issues in research and policy,* edited by L. Goodstein and D. MacKenzie. New York: Plenum, 253–270.

Wright, L.E. and Seymour, C.B. 2000. *Working with children and families separated by incarceration: A handbook for child welfare agencies.* Washington, D.C.: CWLA Press.

Wyatt v. Stickney. 1972.

Zdun, S. 2008. 'Russian' communities in German prisons. *Journal of Scandinavian Studies in Criminology and Crime Prevention,* 9, 42–48

Zilney, L.J. and Zilney, L.A. 2009. *Perverts and Predators: The Making of Sex Offender Laws.* Lanham, MA: Rowman and Littlefield.

Index